MAINE
NEW HAMPSHIRE
& VERMONT

A Touring Guide

Larry H. Ludmer

HUNTER
PUBLISHING

Hunter Publishing, Inc.
300 Raritan Center Parkway
Edison NJ 08818
(908) 225 1900 Fax (908) 417 0482

ISBN 1-55650-728-3

Cover: Fitzwilliam, New Hampshire
(Fridmar Damm/Leo de Wys Inc.)

Maps: Kim André

Contents

Introduction

Whoever it was that first coined the phrase "good things come in small packages" might have been thinking about Maine, New Hampshire and Vermont. New Hampshire ranks 44th in size among the 50 states and Vermont is a step ahead at 43rd. The giant of the three, Maine, although nearly twice the size of the other two combined, comes in 39th. Indeed, if all three states were combined into one, the new entity would still rank 30th. But don't let size fool you. There's plenty of scenery, history and recreation packed into America's most northeasterly corner and the unique New England small town flavor that permeates the region is an additional asset. Because of their small size, all three of these states are among the easiest to see in a single journey, although return trips are always necessary to truly appreciate any place.

Maine is synonymous with great food – especially lobster. Because of its highly irregular shore, it has the second longest coastline on the eastern seaboard. That seacoast is also the east's most dramatic; many people favorably compare it to the coasts of California and Oregon in natural beauty.

New Hampshire rises from a small coastal section to the heights of the White Mountains, with many of the highest peaks in the East. Rising from narrow valleys and lake-studded lowlands, these mountains appear even higher. While they're only a third as high as many of the Rockies, they help create an area of outstanding beauty that attracts hoards of visitors year after year.

Vermont is the only land-locked member of this trio. Mountains dominate the landscape from one end of the state to the other. Nowhere in New England is the small town flavor more pronounced than in this thickly forested state.

The people of these states are alike in many ways. They are fiercely independent, staunchly conservative and protective of their way of life (the American way of life as they see it), proud to share the beauty and history of their states with you.

Getting Started

The chapters are arranged in three roughly circular tours, one for each state. Each route covers dozens of major attractions and many smaller, often lesser-known ones. The suggested itinerary for Maine covers approximately 925 miles, while those for New Hampshire and Vermont are approximately 725 and 600 miles respectively.

Additional attractions will be described that aren't on the main route. For Maine, we offer five different side trips in addition to a small section on other attractions. No sight in either New Hampshire or Vermont is more than 30 miles from the main route, and the majority of those in Maine fall into that category as well.

Don't feel restricted by the suggested route. In any of these states you could select a centrally located town and use that as a base for day or overnight trips to virtually any corner of the state. There are many ways to tour northern New England. The suggested itinerary is simply a convenient framework for you to begin with.

When to Go

The region is well known for its excellent winter skiing. However, we're going to assume that your primary purpose in visiting is not for a ski vacation. Therefore, you wouldn't want to plan on being here during the cold and often stormy winters, when most attractions are closed.

In summer, pleasantly cool days and crisp nights predominate, although it's somewhat warmer along the coast (many people even find the courage to go swimming in the chilly Atlantic). Temperatures at higher altitudes in the Green and White Mountains are cooler than at the lower elevations. Mount Washington is notorious for cold and foul weather year-round.

Spring and fall are, of course, cooler. Some people might find these seasons a little uncomfortable for outdoor activities, but they're worth considering for two reasons. First, there are fewer crowds. Second, and much more important, the brilliant New England foliage season will be a sight that you'll never forget. World-renowned as the best example of nature's fall colors, the exact time varies from year to year depending upon short-term weather trends. Usually, the color change begins on the mountaintops from early to mid-September. The colors reach their peak in late September to early October in the northern portion of these states and in early to mid-October in the south. State tourism offices can give you updated information during the course of the season. It's worth enduring lower temperatures to see the brilliant array of vivid reds, glowing yellows, purples, oranges and other shades. Just keep in mind, again, that some tourist attractions will have reduced operating hours or be closed by the time the peak fall foliage season rolls around.

Be prepared for rain at any time. Dress practically and always pack a sweater and jacket, even in the middle of summer. Although some upscale restaurants still insist on "proper" dress at dinner, a casual style prevails. Be comfortable. Which reminds us to remind you to pack light. It's no fun dragging around a ton of luggage, and you'll find little need to show off your gorgeous wardrobe to the locals. Insect repellent is a good idea if you plan to do a lot of walking in the woods, and sun screen is too. Athough it's rarely hot in summer, the sun can be very strong.

The following chart will give you an idea of the average temperatures and rainfall at various times of the year:

	January			April			July			October		
Location	Hi	Lo	Rain	Hi	Lo	Rain	Hi	Lo	Rain	Hi	Lo	Rain
Portland	32	12	4.4"	53	32	3.8"	80	57	2.8"	60	37	3.0"
Concord	32	11	2.9"	56	32	3.1"	83	56	3.6"	62	36	2.8"
Mt. Washington	12	-2	5.1"	29	15	5.9"	56	42	6.4"	39	25	5.9"
Burlington	27	9	1.9"	53	33	2.6"	82	59	3.7"	57	39	2.9"

Time Allotment

No two people want to spend the same amount of time seeing a given list of attractions. But we do suggest a time frame of about nine days for each of the three main itineraries. You could easily spend much longer or, if pressed for time, squeeze it into fewer days. The nine-day guideline is based on the following assumptions:

- No more than 150 miles of travel on any given day.
- An activity day beginning around 8 each morning and ending at 5 in the afternoon.
- A "fast-food" or other fairly quick lunch.
- Sightseeing times at each attraction as described in the chapters.

If no time is indicated, we anticipate a visit will take under a half-hour. Summertime hours of operation can be found in the Quick Reference Attraction Index at the end of this book.

Although all three states have their share of Interstates, primarily traversing each state from north to south, much of your trip will be on slower state routes and back country roads. The region is mountainous, but there is little mountain driving along the main route. Still, you should never assume that you will average more than about 35 to 40 miles per hour, except when you are on an Interstate.

Lodging and Dining

We don't intend to tell you where to stay or the types of food to eat. Our objective is to help you decide where to stay based on your own preferences. To that end we'll provide information on areas with the greatest variety in lodging and dining along your route. The Addendum provides a listing of the major chain motel locations. Despite the popularity of bed & breakfasts and other alternatives, most people still prefer regular hotel or motel accommodations. Those seeking campgrounds should make inquiry to state tourist offices or consult one of the many commercial campground directories.

For further information, AAA Tourbooks provide one of the most comprehensive listings of lodging and dining establishments. They're updated each year and there is a separate guide published for the states covered in this book. The Tourbooks are free to AAA members at any club office and are available for sale to non-members. Mobil Travel Guides are also a good, if less comprehensive, source. You need the Northeast edition, which is available in bookstores and most libraries. You can also get complete directories for each lodging chain by calling their toll-free reservation number (listed in the Addendum).

The above sources include, besides hotels, motels and resorts, many bed & breakfasts – which originated in New England and remain more popular here than in most other parts of the country. Even longer listings are given by state tourism offices, but they lack the objective evaluations found in independent guidebooks.

Pre-Planned vs. Day-to-Day Approach

There are two possible approaches to any sightseeing trip. You can carefully plan each day, allocating a certain amount of time for traveling, seeing various attractions, and ending the day in a pre-determined place with a room waiting for you. Or you can take things as they come, spending as little or as much time in each place as you want and, when ready, find a place for the night.

When you have a pre-planned itinerary you can be reasonably certain of accomplishing most of what you set out to do. This is important if you, like most people, have limited vacation time and want to get the most out of it. With advance hotel reservations, you won't waste time looking for a place to stay. "No vacancy" signs can be a real problem in out-of-the-way places or small New England towns where rooms are few and are quickly gobbled up. The advantage of the day-to-day approach is its flexibility. Enjoying a particular place? Then stay a little (or a lot) longer. For many travelers the planning stage is fun – it whets the appetite for the real thing. Others have difficulty in figuring out an itinerary and estimating how long to allow for this or that segment of the trip. If you are good at planning, or even if you aren't, this book will provide the means for developing a successful plan, whether you follow the suggested routes to the letter or not.

You can combine the two approaches to some degree. Here's how to do it. Decide where to spend each night based on the amount of mileage you want to cover each day. Don't allocate a specific amount of time for each attraction on the route for that day. Use the ad hoc approach. There is some risk that you'll run out of time on any given day but, if you do, you'll still have spent the most time at the attractions you enjoyed. On the other hand, if nothing appeals to you early in the day, you can almost always find something else to add on, so you won't risk getting to your destination at two o'clock in the afternoon with nothing else to do.

We also previously mentioned that, because of the limited distances involved in these states (especially New Hampshire and Vermont), you may want to stay in one central location and explore the state from that point, returning there for several nights before moving on to the next central location. This method can be used successfully in both the pre-planned and day-to-day approaches.

Some Final Words

The suggested itineraries for each state begin, respectively, in Portland, Manchester and Burlington, because they are the largest cities in this region of mostly small towns. As you will see in the chapters that follow, each itinerary can be joined at numerous points, so the starting point doesn't really matter. Join the route at the point closest to where you're driving from. If you plan on flying into New England, the three cities mentioned above will most likely have to be reached by one or more connecting flights, often by commuter airlines. If you fly into Boston, you will find a much wider choice of flights on regular carriers. Rental car options are also more plentiful in Boston. Furthermore, Boston is only 40 miles from the closest part of the New Hampshire loop, 90 miles from the one for Maine and about 120 from the nearest intersection of the Vermont suggested itinerary. Thus, flying into Boston puts you within easy reach of all three routes.

If you are taking a "fly/drive" trip, remember that the lowest airline fares apply to round-trip flights. Similarly, car rentals are less expensive if you return your vehicle to the renting station. One-way drop-off fees are often high, if the privilege is offered at all. Local car rental companies frequently have lower rates than the major national chains. So do try to make a loop even if you are not going to be doing the entire itinerary outlined here. Again, you may well find that Boston provides a more economical point to start and end your "fly/drive" vacation.

No matter how carefully you plan, there is always the chance that you will get lost at some point. If you have good maps, the chance of that happening will be minimal. The three state maps in this book are designed to provide an overall picture of your trip. Do not rely on them to find your way around. Bring a map of each state that you will be visiting (either AAA maps, which are among the best, or the official highway maps available from each state). These should be supplemented with detailed city maps if you are heading into larger urban areas. Even though northern New England's cities are small, it's much easier to get lost there than on the open road. There are few large National Park areas in this region, but a detailed map of Acadia National Park from the Park Service is recommended if you're visiting Maine, and maps of the several National Forests are also helpful. Contact numbers are given at the end of the book. We're now ready to begin our journey!

Maine

Land of Dramatic Seascapes

Maine has been one of the premier vacation destinations of the country for a long time. Just what gives it such allure for so many people? There is no single answer, for Maine is a land of diverse beauty. Forests, lakes, mountains and picturesque villages all play a big part, but perhaps nothing can quite compare with its famous seacoasts. From fine white sand beaches along the southern coast to the rocky cliffs of Acadia, the Maine seacoast is a vacation wonderland. Stretching for about 230 miles in a straight line from north to south, the coastline is so irregular that the actual distance, including all of its indentations and offshore islands, measures almost 3,500 miles!

Rugged mountains dominate the north-central part of the state. The highest peak is Mt. Katahdin at 5,268 feet. It's located in Baxter State Park, a vast wilderness of forests and lakes. In addition to Mt. Katahdin, Maine has almost 100 peaks that exceed 3,000 feet in elevation, mostly in the Longfellow Mountains.

Famous for potatoes and lobster (although fish and seafood of all types are abundant), Maine has a wealth of outdoor recreational opportunities. Add that to a host of historic attractions and you can begin to understand its popularity. But we've deliberately over-looked another factor up to this point – the Maine way of life, far from the frantic pace of the the cities that lie to the south.

Along the Suggested Itinerary

Portland, as the largest city, is our starting point. Major airlines that come into Portland include Continental, Delta, United and USAir. Or you can fly into Boston's Logan Airport, only about 60 miles from the Maine border via I-93 and I-95. From there you can join the loop described in this chapter at Kittery, just across the Salmon Falls River from New Hampshire. If you're driving in from outside

New England, you'll probably use I-95. If that's the case, pick up the itinerary at that point and continue. For now, we'll begin at Portland and work our way south to Kittery. If you're flying into Portland, the International Jetport is only two miles west of downtown via Congress Street, which is also SR 22 ("SR" refers to "State Route" throughout the remainder of this book).

Portland is Maine's largest city, though its population is less than 75,000. Most major attractions are located within a peninsula that is surrounded by Casco Bay, the Fore River and Back Cove. The area, less than two miles long and a mile wide, contains Portland's downtown. Commercial Street, along the waterfront, Congress Street and Cumberland Avenue are the major north/south thoroughfares, while Franklin, Exchange and High Streets run across.

A good place to start is in the waterfront area known as the **Old Port Exchange**. An integral part of the city's seafaring history, it is now full of shops and restaurants housed in Victorian-style warehouses and other commercial structures. The atmosphere is enhanced by old-style streetlamps and cobblestone streets. A highlight is the huge mural entitled "The Whaling Wall," located at the Maine State Pier on Commercial Street. Almost 1,000 feet long, the mural depicts the variety of sea life found in Maine's coastal waters.

The **Portland Museum of Art** (7 Congress Square) has a large collection of 19th- and 20th-century paintings and sculptures. Many artists who called Maine home are showcased. Adjacent to the art museum is the **Children's Museum of Maine**. The exhibits cover both the physical and social sciences and are geared for those under 10 years of age, so you can reward the little ones for behaving at the Art Museum by taking them here afterwards. Allow about 45 minutes for each.

A block away at 487 Congress Street is the **Wadsworth-Longfellow House**. The home was built by the grandfather of Henry Wadsworth Longfellow in 1785 and was the childhood home of the poet. Within the house are many original furnishings and possessions of the Wadsworth and Longfellow families. The Maine Historical Society Library is on the grounds. Surrounding the house is a small but lovely garden that features large elm trees, lilacs and roses. The nearby **Victoria Mansion** (Danfort Street between High and State) is a mid-19th-century Italian style villa with sumptuous interior decor that uses heavy use of rich woods, marble and porcelain. Each of these homes will require another 45 minutes of your time. A third area mansion is the **Neal Dow Memorial** (714 Congress Street), dating from about 1830. Dow was a local politician and noted supporter of prohibition. Now the house serves as state headquarters of the Christian Temperance Union! Your visit will be confined to the first floor, which contains original furnishings as well as exhibits on Dow's career.

The final structure in the downtown peninsula worth visiting is the **Portland Observatory**, also on Congress. The tower was built in the beginning of the 19th century as a place for the wives of seafarers to watch for the return of their loved ones. Today, it's an excellent place to view the harbor and bay. When the weather is clear you can see as far as New Hampshire's White Mountains. Another good vantage point for viewing Casco Bay is from the Fort Allen Park at the tip of the peninsula on Eastern Promenade, just a couple of blocks from the Observatory.

No visit to Portland is complete without a boat ride on Casco Bay. Both **Bay View Cruises** and **Casco Bay Lines** (both on Commercial Street) offer a variety of tours lasting from an hour to almost three hours. Besides a harbor tour, the picturesque **Calendar Islands** are highlighted on all of the cruises. So named because it was thought there must be one for each day of the year (actually there are 136), these very small islands are tranquil, wooded retreats. **Peaks** and **Great Chebeague Islands** are two of the more popular ones that can be visited (use the tour boats as ferries, just as the locals do).

A number of attractions lie outside the downtown peninsula. Just to the north on the campus of the University of Southern Maine is the **Southworth Planetarium** (Falmouth Street, reached from downtown via State Street into Forest Avenue). There's an exhibit describing our solar system, as well as changing planetarium shows. Allow about a half-hour for the exhibits, twice that if you're going to see a show.

Two miles west of downtown via SR 22 to Westbrook Street is the **Tate House**. The builder of the 1750's house was a representative of the British government and he decorated the interior to resemble a London townhouse. Obviously homesick for the more civilized life of the mother country, Tate included a number of interesting architectural features such as the unusual roof and stairway. Allow between 30 and 45 minutes.

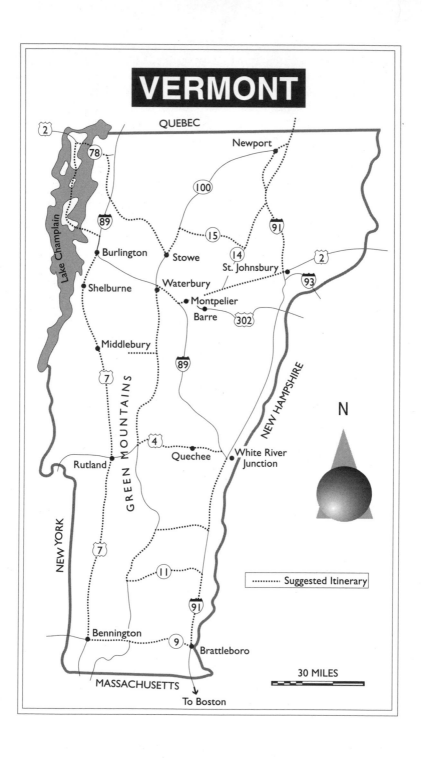

There are also some worthwhile attractions south of downtown, outside Portland's city limits. Follow Broadway east from Portland to South Portland and the Southern Maine Technical College, home of the **Spring Point Museum**. The museum was originally designed to concentrate on the history of Casco Bay, but the current highlight may be the restoration being done on the bow section of an old clipper ship.

SR 77 leads further south from South Portland to nearby Cape Elizabeth. Here are **Two Lights State Park** and the **Portland Head Light**. The former is at the entrance to Casco Bay and provides outstanding views of the Bay and the rocky headlands that surround it. The lighthouse at Portland Head is Maine's oldest, constructed in 1791, and is still in use. There is a museum depicting the long and colorful history of the light and the area has many walking paths offering splendid views, especially of Portland's harbor. Allow approximately a half-hour for the light.

> *Portland has an abundance of places to stay, including most of the major chain hotels, something that is much harder to find in Maine's smaller villages and towns. Restaurants run the gamut from ethnic and home-style to seafood and lobster houses. For shopping you can try the shops in the Old Port Exchange area, or visit the Knightville or Mill Creek shopping areas in South Portland.*

From South Portland, take US 1 southbound. If you're coming directly from Portland, I-295 south will take you to US 1. Go as far as the junction of SR 9 and take Pine Point Road a half-mile east to the **Scarborough Marsh Nature Center**. The more than 3,000 acres of tidal and fresh-water marsh found here are representative of many such areas along the southern Maine coast. There's a variety of wildlife and flora that can be observed from the Marsh Nature Trail. There are guided tours or you can explore at your own pace. Information is available at the Visitor Center. Rent a canoe and see the marsh up close. Allow an hour – longer if you're canoeing or taking a guided tour.

Continue on SR 9 from Scarborough to the next town, **Old Orchard Beach**. This popular resort is known for its white sand beach, some six miles long and 400-700 feet wide. The town, because of the beach's popularity, has become known as a place for fine dining and amusement arcades. It's touristy, but the beach is beautiful, whether you want to go for a swim or simply contemplate the scene. Its mild surf makes it a good choice for children. A nice drive is to follow SR 9 along the Atlantic coast through Orchard Beach and then up along the Saco River, which will bring you into the town of Saco after a mile. The Saco River and Bay are popular for all types of water sports and beach activities. Most of the commercial attractions in town are also water-related. These include the **Aquaboggen Water Park** and the **Cascade Water and Amusement Park**, both on US 1. They have a variety of get-wet rides that are especially popular with children and can keep them amused for several hours. On a more educational plane, the **Marine Aquarium**, also on US 1, has displays featuring hundreds of fish species from all over the world. There are also the usual displays of seals and penguins, as well as a tidal pool. Allow about one hour.

Local and state history are on display in town on Main Street at the **Dyer Library and York Institute Museum**. The two adjacent buildings contain records and artifacts along with furniture dating from as far back as the late 1700s.

Across the Saco River are the towns of **Biddeford** (beginning along US 1), and **Biddeford Pool** (at the coast via SR 9 from Biddeford). Both towns are, more or less, continuations of the resort area that began at Old Orchard Beach and feature the same opportunities for recreation. The **East Point Sanctuary**, at the tip of Biddeford Pool, is a coastal headland area where opportunities for bird watching are excellent. A trail leads you to vantage points where you can observe dozens of different species, including those found in colonies on two small rocky islands just off the coast. Allow a minimum of a half-hour.

> *All of the coastal towns mentioned so far have lodging available, as well as a good choice of dining facilities. This will remain true all the way down the Maine coast as far as Kittery.*

From Biddeford, head south on US 1 for eight miles until the town of Kennebunk. Even better known, Kennebunkport lies four miles west towards the ocean along Port Road (SR's 9A and 35). These towns, along with adjacent Kennebunk Beach, are, in the words of the local residents, "popular with summer folk." Those folks include former President Bush. The entire area has excellent beaches, rocky coasts and extensive forest lands just inland from the shoreline. Picturesque harbor towns are busy places with meticulously-kept stately old homes and quiet streets. Especially popular for shopping is Kennebunkport's restored **Dock Square**. Also in town are the **Kennebunkport Maritime Museum and Gallery** (on Ocean Avenue) and the **Seashore Trolley Museum** (Log Cabin Road). The Maritime Museum is in a former boathouse once owned by the author Booth Tarkington. It features remains of his schooner, *Regina,* and other seafaring artifacts. The Trolley Museum contains one of the country's outstanding collections of electric trolleys. Almost 60 refurbished specimens have been brought here from many cities in the United States, as well as from Europe, Australia and Japan. One of the most popular with visitors is the New Orleans "Streetcar Named Desire." Visitors can observe activities in the restoration shop and take a four-mile trolley ride. Allow about 90 minutes to visit the Trolley Museum. The **Brick Store Museum** in Kennebunk (Main Street) comprises four commercial structures from the early 19th century. Interiors feature local history. Allow 45 minutes to an hour for seeing all of the buildings.

About five miles south of Kennebunk via US 1 is **Wells,** another resort town with miles of ocean beach and plenty of shops. Wells has several attractions. The best known is probably the **Wells Auto Museum**, right on US 1, with a collection of more than a hundred classic cars going back as far as the turn of the century. The newest are from the 1960s. Nickelodians and old-time arcade games are also featured. You can even take a ride in a Model T Ford. Allow between 45 minutes and an hour to explore the museum.

Two natural attractions are the **Rachel Carson National Wildlife Refuge** (north of town on SR 9) and the **Wells National Estuarine Research Reserve** (about two miles from US 1 via Laudholm Farm Road). The Refuge is a preserve of almost 5,000 acres for migratory birds and year-round resident wildlife. A trail extends about a mile through the Refuge. Allow at least a half-hour. The Research Reserve covers 1,600 acres and contains an extensive system of trails through beach, marsh and upland areas. A visitor center provides information on trails and other activities. Allow at least an hour, much more if you're going to be doing several trails.

A few miles south of Wells, again via US 1, is yet another popular beach resort, **Ogunquit**. The name is appropriate; it means "beautiful place by the sea" in the language of the native inhabitants of the area. The town contains numerous shops and art galleries. It is one of many Maine coastal communities that have become artists' colonies. Marginal Way is a footpath extending for about a mile and containing many of the town's shops. Nature's artistry is on display at **Bald Head Cliff**, just south of town via Shore Road. The rocky cliff, one of many in the area, is most notable because of its size – about 100 feet high and extending almost 300 feet into the sea. Huge ocean sprays can often be seen as the tides pound the rock.

Two cruise lines offer scenic trips of one to three hours. These are **Finestkind Scenic Cruises** and the *Silverlining*, both departing from Perkins Cove at the end of Marginal Way. One option available on Finestkind is to take a lobster boat cruise, which includes a lobstering demonstration. Landlubbers might enjoy a visit to the **Ogunquit Museum of American Art** on Shore Road overlooking the ocean. The works of 20th-century American painters are featured. Allow about a half-hour, more if you're an art enthusiast, as the collection is fairly substantial.

The Yorks, comprising the towns of York, York Beach and York Harbor, are five miles south of Ogunquit via US 1. (Note that I-95, the Maine Turnpike, parallels US 1 along the entire southern Maine coast, but you'll spend as much time getting on and off the toll-road as you will by remaining on the "slower" US 1.)

Historic York was given a Royal Colony status as early as 1641 and was the very first chartered city in America. An interesting historic district is centered around the junction of US 1A (Main Street) and Lindsay Road. About a half-dozen buildings comprise **Old York**, representing the development of York from the 18th through the early 20th centuries. There are both guided and self-guided tours available for two old houses, a schoolhouse, commercial warehouse, the Jefferd's Tavern and the Old Gaol (used as a jail until the mid-19th century). Built in 1719, it is one of the oldest public buildings in the United States still standing. Give yourself about 90 minutes to tour Old York. Continue on US 1A from York Village to the town of **York Harbor**. This scenic two-mile drive follows the shoreline into the heart of this oceanfront resort community, once frequented by the richest families of the East and now available to everyone. The busy harbor area is popular with visitors for its shops and restaurants. Take a walk over the 19th-century Wrigley Bridge, which crosses the York River, for a good view. On the north side of town a small rocky headland extends into the ocean; called

Cape Neddick, it is known for the famous and much-photo-graphed **Cape Neddick Lighthouse**, often referred to by locals as the Nubble Light. The lighthouse stands atop a tiny island off the end of Cape Neddick.

Proceeding south once again on US 1, it's about seven miles from York to Maine's most southerly community, **Kittery**, which provides views of New Hampshire's Portsmouth Harbor. The best place to see the harbor is from the remains of **Fort Foster**, a Civil War fortification built on tiny Gerish Island. What's left of the fort is set in an attractive park. Kittery has long been associated with shipbuilding, once for large commercial wooden vessels, and today for smaller pleasure craft. More history is in evidence at the **Fort McClary State Historic Site**, two miles east of town on SR 103. The structures visible today were built in the 1840's. For a better feel of the area's maritime history, take US 1 north to Rogers Road and the **Kittery Historical and Naval Museum**. Allow about 45 minutes to view the exhibits on the town's shipbuilding heritage, which encompasses more than three centuries.

Having reached the southernmost part of the state, we'll now parallel the **Salmon Falls River**, which serves as the border between Maine and New Hampshire, by taking SR 103 westbound for eight miles to the town of South Berwick. Located along the river are the lovely **Vaughan Woods**, 250 acres containing many easy walking trails. According to local lore, a ship named the *Pied Cow* came ashore near this site and brought the first cows to Maine, along with materials to build the first sawmill, which was constructed on a site not far from the Vaughan Woods. Allow a minimum of a half-hour.

South Berwick also has a number of historic homes that can be visited. The two outstanding ones are **Hamilton House** and the **Sarah Orne Jewett House**, both off of SR 236. Each house dates from the late 18th century. The latter is more richly furnished, but Hamilton House has an impressive formal garden with statuary and a sundial bordered by hedges. Stately trees and colorful flower beds adorn meandering pathways. Tours of both houses are given on the hour and take about 30 minutes each. The gardens can be viewed on your own.

From the center of South Berwick, pick up SR 4 and head north 14 miles to the junction of SR 109 in South Sanford. Turn left onto SR 109 and proceed about five miles to SR 11A in the town of

Springvale. Here you'll find the small (about five acres), but out-standing, **Harvey Butler Rhododendron Sanctuary**. Also on the attractively landscraped grounds are trillium and various native wildflowers and black birch trees. However, the rhododendron is the star and is most spectacular in the early part of July. Allow a half-hour.

Now reverse your route on SR 109 for a short distance back to Sanford and take US 202 east (even though you'll actually be traveling north) for about 40 miles to the town of Gray. (A side trip originates from Gorham, about half-way to Gray from Springvale; see the section at the end of this chapter.) Dating from the late 1770's, Gray became the site of several mills in the early part of the 19th century. In town, take SR 26 north to the **Fish and Wildlife Visitors Center**. This interesting facility showcases Maine's native wildlife. Besides viewing informative exhibits, you'll be able to see animals such as moose, deer and bear being cared for. The Center takes in injured or orphaned animals. Give yourself about 45 min-utes here.

Stay on SR 26 north for 10 more miles until you reach the town of Poland Spring. If the name sounds familiar, it's because this is the source of the bottled "Poland Spring Water." The spring itself is now owned by the company that bottles the water and is, unfortu-nately, not open to visitors. However, you can visit the **Maine State Building and All Souls Chapel** (off of SR 26 in town). The struc-ture was Maine's exhibit at Chicago's 1893 Columbian Exposition and was dismantled and reassembled on this site. The major por-tion of the handsome Victorian building contains exhibits on the former Poland Spring Resort, while the chapel features nine beau-tiful stained glass windows. The granite structure also contains Westminster Chimes and recitals are held on Monday evenings. Along SR 26 at Sabbathday Lake is the **Shaker Museum**, which houses artifacts and buildings of the only still-active Shaker relig-ious community in the United States. Allow a minimum of a half-hour.

Continue on SR 26 for four miles to the junction of SR 11 and turn right (unless you're taking the second side trip as described later). Proceed for two miles to the community of Mechanic Falls and turn right on SR 121. Take this road 10 miles to the neighboring towns of **Auburn** and **Lewiston**.

Auburn and Lewiston have the best lodging options of any places since you left Kittery.

The two communites are separated by the Androscoggin River and have long been commercially important. Combined, the region is second to Portland in both population and economic activity. SR 121 becomes Minot Avenue in Auburn and leads downtown. There you should visit the **Androscoggin Historical Society Museum** (Turner and Court Streets). This museum is housed in the County Office Building and describes the history of the entire state, with special emphasis on local events. An interesting collection of artifacts enlivens the displays.

From downtown Auburn take US 202 eastbound. Once across the Longley Bridge spanning the Androscoggin River – where you can catch a brief look at the Lewiston Falls and Dam – the US Highway becomes Main Street. Proceed to Russel Street (about a mile), turn right and go two blocks to the campus of **Bates College**. In the Olin Center there's an art museum featuring the work of local artists and others. However, the highlight of your visit to the school will be a trip to the top of Mount David, located on the campus. It provides an excellent view of the entire Auburn-Lewiston area, the Androscoggin Valley and, on good weather days, vistas of New Hampshire's Presidential Range. Allow at least a half-hour at the campus.

Just east of downtown via Highland Springs Road is the **Thorncrag Bird Sanctuary**. Not only birds but numerous other native species inhabit the sanctuary. Its 200 acres can best be seen from the miles of trails that wind through the forest. Allow at least an hour.

Leave Lewiston via US 202, still heading east. Drive about 16 miles to the town of North Monmouth, then turn right on SR 132 for two miles into Monmouth. This road is Main Street, site of the **Monmouth Museum**. A living history museum, the site contains five different buildings dating back to the 19th century and a residence from the late 18th century. A blacksmith shop and carriage house are among the commercial structures. Both guided and unguided tours are available. Allow at least a half-hour.

Return to US 202 and travel east once again, this time for 12 miles, until you reach the state's capital city – **Augusta**. Set in the middle of the state, Augusta is split into two sections by the Kennebec River. The Statehouse Complex, between State Street and the River, houses most of the city's major points of interest. Begin at the **Statehouse**, built of granite from the nearby town of Hallowell. The structure dates from 1829 and is dominated by the great dome, which can be seen from just about any point within the city. Portraits of famous Maine personages and historic flags adorn the interior. You can take a self-guiding tour through the building, approximately 30 minutes. The capitol building is at one corner of the **Augusta State Park**, more commonly known as the Capitol Park. Containing almost a hundred different species of trees (three-fourths native to Maine), the park is a beautiful adornment to the Statehouse. Here, too, is Maine's state memorial to Vietnam veterans. Also within the Statehouse Complex is the **Maine State Museum**. This outstanding museum depicts the state's history, its resources, people and more in several separate major exhibits – "This Land Called Maine," "12,000 Years in Maine," and "Made in Maine." Give yourself a minimum of an hour to tour the many exhibits.

Tours of the nearby Governor's Mansion (State and Capitol Streets), called **Blaine House**, are periodically available as well. Built in the 1830s, it became the executive mansion in 1919. Even if it's not open to visitors when you're there, do take some time to explore the lovely three-acre grounds. Beautiful flowers and stately trees are arranged in a pattern created by the famous landscape artists, the Olmsted brothers.

The final Augusta attraction of note is the **Fort Western Museum** on the Kennebec (reached via Cony Street). A wooden structure, among the oldest still standing in New England, the fort has been restored to its mid-18th-century appearance. Reenactments of daily activities by costumed guides are given throughout the day. Allow about 45 minutes.

> *Augusta is home to almost a dozen major lodging chains and there's a good assortment of restaurants featuring local and international cuisine.*

To leave Augusta and continue your journey, follow State Street north. It will turn into Mt. Vernon Avenue and will cross I-95 about 2½ miles from the Capitol area. Head north on I-95 and in 15 miles you'll reach the city of **Waterville** (Exit 33). Like the larger Augusta to the south, Waterville is on the Kennebec River, whose navigable status has shaped the history of the area.

Immediately to the west of town on Mayflower Hill is the campus of **Colby College**. The small college was established in 1813 and has an excellent nationwide reputation. The large (more than 700 acres) and beautiful campus contains many fine buildings of varying architectural styles. They are worth taking the time to see by strolling around campus. The college's Museum of Art (Bixler Center) is the most visited structure, but the Miller Library and Lorimer Chapel should also be seen. Although tours of the campus are given, they're more geared towards prospective students. You can take a self-guiding tour, which will last between 30 and 45 minutes. A separate point of interest, although still on campus, is the **Perkins Arboretum and Bird Sanctuary**. Covering almost 130 acres, the sanctuary is a workshop for students studying flora and fauna; but you are free to wander along the sanctuary's many marked trails. Allow close to an hour.

The **Redington Museum** (downtown on Silver Street) recounts Waterville's early days. Recreations of various 19th-century establishments create an authentic atmosphere. Allow 45 minutes to an hour.

Upon leaving Waterville, head north on I-95 again, this time for a couple of miles to Exit 36. This is US 201 and you'll follow it north for 16 miles to the town of Skowhegan. The logging industry is of great importance in the Skowhegan area, a town of almost 9,000 people. There are several places to stay in town and a few attractions, although Skowhegan's major importance to you is as a gateway to the scenic Kennebec Valley, which lies to the north. It's also the starting and ending point for a third sidetrip you might decide to take (described later in the chapter). Skowhegan was the home of one of the Senate's most famous women members – Margaret Chase Smith. You can visit the **Margaret Chase Smith Library**, which chronicles her life. Allow about a half-hour. You should also take a few minutes to view the 62-foot-high sculpture of an Indian, which pays tribute to the area's native Abenaki Indian tribe.

You'll now be traveling north on US 201 for a total distance of 80 miles to the town of Jackman. However, there are many sights along this beautiful route, which has been designated a Maine State Scenic Highway.

The small twin communities of Bingham and Moscow are a half-hour's drive from Skowhegan. In the area are lovely **Houston Brook Falls** and the **Wyman Dam**, which affords outstanding views of Wyman Lake, an impoundment of the Kennebec River. After Moscow the road follows the river for another 25 miles, where it reaches the town of West Forks. The area is known more commonly as "The Forks." Before crossing the highway bridge leading into town take the side road for three miles to **Moxie Falls**. Follow the marked trails to the observation platform, where you get a wonderful view of one of Maine's highest and possibly most beautiful waterfalls. If you're more adventurous, there's a difficult trail leading from the platform area to near the base of the falls. This is a strenuous hike and may not be for everyone, but if you're in decent shape you should be able to accomplish the complete trip in a little over an hour. Otherwise, to view the falls, allow about 30 minutes for the round-trip.

The Forks is a popular spot for whitewater rafting through beautiful gorges. A dozen or so operators line the main street in town. (See Addendum 3 for a partial listing.) Most trips range from a couple of hours to a half-day, but multi-day excursions are available for those with plenty of time to spend in the wild.

As US 201 heads away from the Kennebec River on its final leg toward Jackman (accommodations are generally simple, but plentiful), you'll be traveling through part of a 250,000-acre wilderness area. The scenery encompasses lakes and ponds, forests and more. Recreational opportunities for fishing and boating are plentiful.

At Jackman, US 201 heads north to the Canadian province of Quebec. However, we'll be heading east on SR 6, traveling for 50 miles to the town of Greenville. The ride is a most pleasant one – little traffic and excellent views of, first, Brassue Lake and then the much larger Moosehead Lake.

> *Greenville has a number of motels and restaurants that make it attractive as a place to spend the night.*

Greenville's attractions are related primarily to its location at the southernmost point on Moosehead Lake. Some of the surrounding rivers are good places for whitewater rafting. Inquire in town regarding local outfitters. A more sedate pastime is to take a cruise on the lake via the *Katahdin*, a 1914 lake steamer that has been beautifully restored at a cost of over a half-million dollars. Cruises last 2½ hours. What makes this boat ride unusual is that a portion of the *Katahdin* has been set aside as the **Moosehead Marine Museum**, so if you feel like diverting your attention from the lovely scenery for a few minutes you can explore a gallery devoted to the ships that have sailed Moosehead Lake over the years. The museum can also be visited when the ship is in port should you not want to take the cruise.

Upon leaving Greenville you'll begin the longest part of the suggested itinerary without stops for attractions. Heading for Calais, a distance of 162 miles, stay on US 6 westbound for 125 miles to the town of Topsfield, then turn onto US 1 south for the remainder of the journey into Calais. Although it's not that long a trip, you might be able to break up the ride by staying overnight along the route, depending upon the time of day you're in the area.

> *The town of Lincoln, a bit more than halfway to Calais, has the greatest number of hotels.*

The scenery en route is pleasant enough, comprising distant mountains, rivers and lakes and the ever-present forest. Where the route crosses I-95 is the starting point for two more optional side trips that are discussed later. The drive to Calais, without stops, will take under four hours.

Migratory birds pass over **Calais** on their north-south treks. It was settled in 1770 and is connected to Canada via the International Bridge across the St. Croix River. The **Moosehorn National Wildlife Refuge** just outside of town is a good place to view many varieties of waterfowl. The 12,000-acre section of the refuge closest to town contains both short nature trails and longer hiking trails through the woods. Allow a minimum of 45 minutes and longer if you plan to do any extensive hiking.

> *Calais is home to a number of good motels.*

The town of Calais is at the head of Passamaquoddy Bay, and you'll be traveling along its western shore as you head further south on US 1. Twenty miles south of Calais, turn onto SR 190. This road only goes for seven miles, ending at the scenic town of Eastport on a peninsula separating Passamaquoddy and Cobscook Bays. **Eastport**, with a population of about 2,000, has the distinction of being America's easternmost city. One of the world's largest whirlpools is located in the area and occurs two hours before high tide. It is visible from Dog Island via Water Street. Inquire as to tide times at the local Chamber of Commerce. A walk down Water Street is also a stroll through another era, as many former homes of sea captains have been restored. Today, a lot of them are occupied by artists. The **Waponahki Museum** on SR 190 chronicles the history of the Passamaquoddy Indians, the original inhabitants of the area. Allow 30-45 minutes.

Head back on SR 190 to US 1 and turn left, continuing south as the highway loops around the winding shore of Cobscook Bay. A little over 20 miles after rejoining US 1 you'll reach the town of Whiting. Pick up SR 189, which begins in town, and take it to Lubec, a distance of about 12 miles. **Lubec**, about the same size as Eastport, is only a couple of miles from the latter if you cross the Bay by boat, even though you had to travel almost 40 miles to get here by road. The town is also on a peninsula and, being the easternmost point in the country, is the spot where the sun rises first on the United States! It is separated from Canada's Campobello Island by the Lubec Narrows via the Franklin D. Roosevelt Memorial Bridge. The island is where the President spent most of his summers as a child and young man. The **Roosevelt Campobello International Park** is a joint American and Canadian tribute to his memory. You can walk more than eight miles of nature trails through the woods and tour the 34-room house where the Roosevelt family lived. Allow about 45 minutes to visit the house and another 30 minutes or more to explore the grounds. Actually, as the estate covers over 2,600 acres, you could spend hours wandering the tranquil surroundings.

To the immediate south of town is the **Quoddy Head State Park**. An old lighthouse built in the early 1800s is on the site; although not open to the public, it makes a picturesque place to view some of the very rocky cliffs, many of which tower almost 100 feet above the pounding ocean surf. Whale-watching from Quoddy Head is also a popular activity. The nearby West Quoddy Marine Research Station has exhibits on whales and can provide information on the best times to observe these animals.

Leave Lubec the opposite way you entered, working your way back to US 1 and proceeding south for a short time until you reach the tri-community of **East Machias, Machias** and **Machiasport.**

> *You will find the best choice of accommodations and dining in Machias proper.*

The towns surround Machias Bay and, like so many other Maine communities, provide opportunities to see the rugged coast dotted with small islands. In Machias (off Main Street) the Machias River tumbles through an impressive gorge. The towns date from the 18th century and are rich in Revolutionary War era history. The first naval battle of the war occured on Machias Bay. Visitors should plan on seeing the **Burnham Tavern Museum** (Machias, on Main Street), which houses a collection of 18th-century artifacts, and the **Gates House** (Machiasport, on SR 92). Similar in scope to the Burnham Tavern, the latter also has models of the ships that took part in the first naval engagement of the Revolution. Allow about an hour to complete your visit to both museums.

A little less than 20 miles south of Machias, again via US 1, you'll reach **Columbia Falls**, a tiny community with only 600 residents. Once an important shipbuilding center, the town is much quieter today. However, you can stop in at the **Ruggles House**, the former residence of an important local businessman and military official. The house is astonishing for two reasons – first, the "flying staircase," which seems to rise without any visible means of support and, second, the intricate carvings on both the wooden interior and exterior. It is believed that the carvings were made using only a penknife. Allow about a half-hour to see the house.

Shortly after Columbia Falls, US 1 passes through the Cherryfield area, an especially attractive portion of the route along the Narraguagus River. Stay on US 1 until the town of Gouldsboro and then travel south on SR 186 for eight miles. You will pass Birch Harbor and reach a one-way road that circles the Schoodic Peninsula.. The peninsula is part of Acadia National Park, the main portion of which will be described shortly. It is only about an hour's drive from here. The peninsula's main attraction is **Schoodic Point**, which juts further into the Atlantic than any other part of the east coast, and its beautifully rugged granite rock called Schoodic Head. This outcropping rises more than 400 feet and provides outstanding views. Excellent vistas of the Bay of Fundy and the peaks of Mount Desert Island (where Acadia National Park proper is located) are available from just about anywhere on Schoodic Point. The road follows near the edge of the peninsula, circling the entire Point and returning to SR 186 and then continuing on to US 1 north of the town of Winter Harbor.

Once you return to US 1, turn left and travel for 17 miles to the junction of SR 3, just before the town of Ellsworth. Then turn south on SR 3 and in a few minutes you'll cross a bridge over the Mt. Desert Narrows, which separates the mainland from the unusually shaped Mt. Desert Island. Once across the bridge, stay on SR 3 and in a couple of miles you'll pass through the entrance station of **Acadia National Park** and find yourself at the Visitor Center.

Acadia was established in 1919 and its nearly 40,000 acres cover the greater portion of Mt. Desert Island. Like most National Parks, Acadia is a vast area of pristine land set aside to preserve a special area of natural beauty – in this case, the most famous example of rugged coastline in the east. One of only a handful of National Parks in the east, Acadia is different in another way – within the park's borders are numerous areas of land that are privately owned. Please respect private property at all times. On the plus side, the private lands include communities that provide a break from touring and that have an abundance of good restaurants and lodging. The largest ones are Bar Harbor and Northeast Harbor.

The cliffs of Acadia are justly the most famous of all Maine's rocky shores. The relentless pounding of the surf wears away at the cliff bottoms. But Acadia is more than just a series of rocky promontories. Forest-covered Mt. Desert Island contains Cadillac Mountain, the highest point on the Atlantic seaboard. A variety of flora and fauna grace the park from end to end.

Begin your tour at the modern and large Hull Cove Visitor Center, where exhibits will acquaint you with the natural and human history of Acadia. The 27-mile-long Park Loop Road begins at the Visitor Center. Most of the Loop is one-way, making your driving much easier.

Several miles south of the Visitor Center, after passing by the town of Bar Harbor, is the Sieur de Monts Springs area. The small Abbe Museum contains Indian artifacts, but the Nature Center trail and the Acadia Wild Garden are of greater interest. Hilly paths wind through more than 400 different species of plants and flowers. Soon afterward, the road reaches the ocean cliffs and begins the greatest concentration of scenery in all of Acadia. Great Head, one of the largest rocky headlands anywhere, is first and is followed quickly by Sand Beach, composed primarily of tiny fragments of crushed seashells. Then comes one of the main stars of Acadia, Thunder Hole. Here you'll look into the gorge-like crevice of one of the many sea cliffs and see the waves crashing. When the tidal conditions are right the surf creates a mighty roar that sounds a lot like thunder. Even without the added noise it's quite a sight. Soon after Thunder Hole come the Otter Cliffs, where Acadia's thick forest comes down from the mountains almost to the very edge of the cliffs, which tower more than 100 feet above the ocean.

At the town of Seal Harbor the road turns north. After passing Jordan Pond and Eagle Lake there is a side road to the summit of Cadillac Mountain. You might want to stop for lunch or afternoon tea at Jordan Pond House. The round-trip is about seven miles from the main Park Loop Road and is worth far more than the few minutes it takes to reach the mountaintop – you'll have a panorama in every direction, seeing all of Mt. Desert Island, the many towns of the island as well as the nearby mainland, the ocean with its many small offshore islands and the beautiful rocky cliffs. An excellent overlook is about half-way up. Many trails begin at the summit itself. It's a sight you'll long remember.

Return to the main road and backtrack (this portion of the loop is two-way) to Seal Harbor, and on to Northeast Harbor. Continue on SR 3 (also SR 198) to the junction of SR 102. Turn left onto SR 102. Here, a second loop begins that covers the southwest section of the island. The scenery on this stretch is not nearly as dramatic as that which you have just covered but, beginning with Southwest Harbor, almost a dozen picturesque seaside towns dot the landscape.

Acadia National Park, in addition to the Park Loop Road, is traversed by more than 120 miles of trails and over 50 miles of "carriage roads." The latter are so named because during the early part of the century visitors would tour the area by horse-drawn carriage. Actually, you can still do this; carriage rides can still be arranged at Wildwood Stables in the park (call 207-276-3622); they are located near Jordan Pond House and are open from Memorial Day until Columbus Day. You can also walk or bicycle on the carriage roads so they make a remarkably easy way to tour the interior of Mt. Desert Island. Bicycle rentals are available in Bar Harbor, Northeast Harbor and Southwest Harbor.

Allow a minimum of four hours to tour the National Park and much more if you intend to do a lot of exploration on the trails and carriage roads. Complete information and maps are available at the Visitor Center.

Now we'll turn our attention to the towns. **Bar Harbor** is the largest and most popular of the resort towns. Visit the **Mt. Desert Oceanarium**, which contains a 50,000 gallon seal tank and a walk through a marshland ecosystem, as well as other exhibits. There's also a lobster fishing demonstration. Allow 60-90 minutes. (There's also a smaller Oceanarium in Southwest Harbor. The exhibits are different and you can cover that one in about a half-hour.) Whale watching is one of the most popular activities in this area and you can leave from Bar Harbor on the *Acadian Whale Watcher* cruise. This is a four-hour journey. Bar Harbor is also home to scores of art galleries and quaint shops.

In **Southwest Harbor** you can tour the **Gilley Museum** (Main Street), which houses a collection of more than 200 hand-carved wooden birds. Mr. Gilley is one of the foremost woodcarvers in the country and has gained national recognition for his skills. Other exhibits about the birds of the region are also of interest.

Finally, the town of **Seal Cove** has an attraction that's a bit different for Mt. Desert Island – the **Seal Cove Auto Museum** (on SR 102) has about a hundred antique cars, some dating from before the turn of the century. Allow about 45 minutes, perhaps more if you're into vintage wheels.

There's only one road onto Mt. Desert Island so you'll be leaving the way you came in, via SR 3. As you reach the mainland the town of Trenton is immediately to your left. The **Acadia Zoo** is a good stop if you have children, since they'll like the petting zoo and animal shows. Adults may enjoy it as well, but it's far from a major zoological garden.

Continue now on SR 3 until you return to US 1. Turn left (south) and in a mile you'll reach Ellsworth. Home to many historic buildings, the first attraction you'll come upon is the **Stanwood Homestead Museum and Bird Sanctuary**. The house belonged to a noted bird expert and contains furnishings from the mid-19th century. Of greater note is the 130-acre sanctuary surrounding the house. It is crossed by numerous paths and is home to many species of birds. Allow about an hour combined for the house and sanctuary.

Another 19th-century structure worth special mention is the **Black House,** which is also furnished in period. A carriage house is especially interesting, as are the formal gardens which surround the mansion.

Upon leaving Ellsworth, US 1 splits with US 1A. Take the 1A fork, which leads 30 miles directly into the city of **Bangor.** With more than 33,000 people, Bangor is one of the state's largest communities, its history rooted in the lumbering industry. Today it's a much more diverse town, with attractive brick-paved streets in the commercial hub centered around Union Street and many shops and restaurants to choose from. There's even an 80-store major retail mall.

Bangor offers numerous motels and hotels in all price ranges.

The **Bangor Historical Society Museum** (on Union Street, downtown) is an 1836 Greek Revival home, a popular style throughout Maine. The house is furnished in period and also serves as the starting point for a walking tour of Bangor's historic area. Brochures for that purpose are available here. Allow about an hour for the home and walking tour. The **Cole Land Transportation Museum** (Perry Road) features land vehicles of every imaginable type, from baby carriages to huge 18-wheeler trucks. The primary thrust of the museum's exhibits, however, is to trace the development of freight transportation. Give yourself about 45 minutes.

Leave Bangor via I-95 heading north. Take it approximately 10 miles to Exit 51 and the town of **Orono.** Situated in the picturesque Penobscot Valley, Orono is known mainly as the home of the **University of Maine.** The 1,200-acre campus is lovely and you can tour the spacious grounds either on foot or by car. A variety of architectural styles show the history of the school since its founding in 1865. The campus is home to the **Maine Center for the Arts,** the state's premier cultural center for plays, concerts and the like. There's also an art museum and several art galleries. Allow about an hour.

Only three miles northeast of Orono is **Old Town,** another lumbering town. Today it's still home to a large number of Penobscot Indians. They reside primarily on an island in the Penobscot River. You can see traditional craft skills practiced here. The **Old Town**

Museum traces the local lumbering industry as well as the Indian heritage of the area. Works by local artists are also on display.

Now make your way back through Orono and Bangor via I-95. From Bangor drive south on US 1A for 20 miles to the town of Prospect and then turn left on SR 174, taking the latter road for two miles to just before the junction of US 1. This will bring you to the entrance of **Fort Knox State Historic Site**. Built in the 1840s out of fear of further British aggression from Canada, the five-sided fort commands a view of the Penobscot River. Not to be confused with the famous gold depository of the same name, this granite Fort Knox's reputation doesn't go as far. It never took part in any hostilities, but a tour of the fort is nonetheless interesting. It's an excellent example of a mid-19th-century garrison. Inquire as to times when Civil War gun demonstrations are given. Otherwise, allow about 30 minutes to tour the fort.

Now take US 1 south for a little more than 10 miles to **Searsport**, another former shipbuilding community with stately old houses lining the streets. The main attraction in town is the **Penobscot Marine Museum** on US 1, comprised of seven buildings from the first half of the 19th century. While the museum's structures occupy the home of a sea captain, a former town hall and other diverse buildings, they all now contain a comprehensive collection of nautical items that fully document the maritime history of Maine, including one of the finest galleries of nautical art. Give yourself a minimum of 90 minutes to cover all of the museum's buildings.

A few miles further south on US 1 is another town with a ship-building heritage – **Belfast**. Elegant old homes are all over this popular artists' colony and lovely shops line Main Street all the way down to the bay and the **Waterfront Heritage Park**, which is devoted to the town's history.

> *There's a good selection of lodging and dining options in Belfast, as well as in Camden, your next destination 20 miles south on US 1.*

US 1 is itself a very scenic road in the area from Searsport all the way to Rockland, a total of almost 40 miles, with excellent views of Penobscot Bay and large North Haven Island.

One of the best views of the area is in **Camden Hills State Park,** two miles north of Camden town. An easy mile-long paved road ascends Mount Battie. From the 900-foot summit you'll have outstanding views of not only the town and its harbor but all of the Bay and, on clear days, even Acadia National Park. A mile south of town is the **Old Conway House and Museum,** an 18th-century farmhouse filled with period furnishings. There's also a barn with displays of sleighs and various farming equipment. Allow about 30 minutes. A final Camden attraction is **Merryspring,** a horticultural exhibit covering almost 70 acres off US 1 on Conway Road and just a stone's throw from the Old Conway House. A diverse collection of plants, flowers and ground covers are spread out along attractive walks. Give yourself another half-hour for the gardens.

Only two miles south of Camden is **Rockport,** and then another six miles brings you to **Rockland.** These are two of Maine's most popular coastal ports.

> *Rockport and Rockland have plenty of places to eat and sleep, although many are in a higher price category than elsewhere.*

Both are also major art communities, especially during the summertime. Indeed, Rockport is the home of the **Maine Coast Artists Gallery** which has changing exhibitions of contemporary Maine artisans. The building is a former livery stable. The amount of time you spend here depends primarily on your interest in art. Adjacent to Rockport's harbor is the **Rockport Marine Park.** A character from a popular series of children's books, Andre the Seal, is commemorated in the park with a statue. Three lime kilns from the turn of the century are also on display, as are copies of steam locomotives formerly used to transport the lime from the kilns to freighters moored in the harbor. Finally, the attractive **Gardens of Vesper Hill Children's Chapel** feature a number of different gardens. The Chapel is a place of meditation and affords an ocean vista. Allow about 30 minutes.

Rockland is the larger of the two communities and is the town where the famous poet Edna St. Vincent Millay was born. Although lobster fishing (and eating) is popular all up and down the coast, Rockland deems itself the "Lobster Capital of the World." There's a major lobster festival during the first week in August. Main Street, lined with many historic buildings, is now the modern shopping hub of the area. Windjammer cruises on the Bay are popular and you can inquire about them from a number of operators along the harborfront.

In connection with the town's significant link to the arts, the **Farnsworth Art Museum** (on Elms Street downtown) has a collection of paintings representing many artists, both American and foreign. However, the major thrust of the museum's works are those artists who had at least some connection with Maine. Allow between 45 minutes and an hour, and a bit more if you're going to visit the Greek-revival style Farnsworth Homestead adjacent to the museum building. It was built in 1850 and contains many original furnishings. The **Owls Head Transportation Museum** (two miles south of town on SR 73) contains a variety of antique conveyances. Allow about 30 minutes.

Lighthouses play an important role in the history of Maine's coast and Rockland is a good place to see and learn about them. The **Shore Village Museum** on Limerock Street contains an impressive collection of Coast Guard equipment including lights, lifesaving apparatus and equipment used in lighthouses. Allow a half-hour. Rockland's lighthouse, sitting almost a mile from town at the end of a breakwater, was built in 1888 and makes an extremely attractive sight.

From Rockland US 1 veers away from the coast a bit, but it's only about four miles to the town of **Thomaston**, your next stop. This is another town with a lively seafaring history and many gracious homes that were once occupied by ship captains. Henry Knox, Secretary of War under President Washington, resided in Thomaston and a replica of his home, **Montpelier**, has been built here. The reproduction of the house is completely authentic and many of the furnishings are original. Montpelier offers guided tours or you can browse on your own. It's at the junction of US 1 and SR 131 and takes about 30 minutes to visit.

About five miles past Thomaston, US 1 reaches the junction of SR 190. Take that road east for one mile to the **Georges River Canal System**, located in Payson Park in the town of Warren. The canal spans almost 30 miles and was built in 1795, making it America's second oldest. There's a bridge crossing the canal and hiking trails through the park.

Return to US 1 south and proceed another seven miles to **Waldoboro**, an attractive town set on an inlet at the head of Muscongus Bay. The **Waldoboro Museum** is housed in three 19th-century buildings on SR 220, about a half-mile south of the main part of town. Exhibits range from household artifacts and Maine crafts to models of ships. There's also an opportunity to view farm animals as the museum's grounds contain a pound for stray animals.

Another 10 miles further south and off US 1 via SR 129 is the community of **Damariscotta** (lodging available). A typical Maine seacoast town if there is one, Damariscotta is another village rich in seafaring history. A variety of cultural events take place at the **Round Top Center for the Arts**. It also houses an art gallery and craft exhibits. The clocktower of the Baptist Church is a noted attraction.

Newcastle is less than a mile away from Damariscotta and is back by US 1. Here you can pay a brief visit to **St. Patrick's Church**. It was built in 1808, making it one of the oldest Catholic churches in New England that is still standing. **St. Andrew's**, an Episcopal Church, was designed by Henry Vaughn, who also designed the National Cathedral in Washington. While not as spectacular as that work, St. Andrew's is a lovely structure worth taking a look at. Newcastle also has a number of elegant old homes that can be seen by taking a stroll down virtually any street in town. Look for the Glidden House, dating from 1752 and the 1800 Kavanaugh Mansion, whose owner was the Governor of Maine in the 1840s.

From Newcastle proceed once again along US 1 southbound, this time for seven miles to the town of **Wiscasset**. Claiming to be Maine's prettiest village (a point that would be argued by residents and supporters of literally hundreds of other villages), Wiscasset is another popular community for artists and writers. There are many old houses, as well as relics of its seafaring tradition – you can see the decaying remains of two schooners that have been left in the harbor since the 1930s, the *Luther Little* and the *Hesprus*. Among the noteworthy homes are the **Castle Tucker House Museum** (High Street) and the **Nickels-Sortwell House** (Main Street). Both date from the early 1800s. Allow about 30 minutes for each.

Wiscassset contains several other worthwhile attractions. These include: **Fort Edgecomb State Historic Site, Old Lincoln County Jail and Museum,** and the **Pownalborough Courthouse**. Fort Edgecomb is about a mile from town, south of US 1. It's an eight-sided wooden fort built in 1809 during the lead-up to war with England that was to come three years later. It gives a good idea of the construction methods used during that era and you can see it in about 30 minutes. The county jail, opened in 1811, was in use for over a hundred years. The granite structure has thick walls, the interior ones still covered with the original grafitti of its occupants. The courthouse (via SR 128) was built in 1761 and houses a furnished courtroom of the period, including the judge's residence. Both of the preceding can be seen in about a half-hour.

On a more current note, the **Maine Yankee Energy Information Center** (via signs following SR 144) teaches visitors about nuclear energy. Participatory exhibits highlight the displays and you can view the exterior of the power plant. Allow about 45 minutes. Back downtown on High Street is the **Musical Wonder House**, containing a large collection of mechanical musical instruments, many European and American music boxes and player pianos. Give yourself at least 45 minutes to view the unusual items here.

Finally, Wiscasset offers both train and boat rides along the lovely Sheepscot River. Both depart from Water Street via the **Maine Coast Navigation and Railroad**. The train ride is on restored passenger coaches from the 1930s and the boat ride is on the *Islander II*. Wildlife can be seen on both trips, but especially on the boat, which also sails past Fort Edgecomb. Each trip lasts 75 minutes. If you only have time for one, the boat ride is highly recommended, although there's a discount if you take both.

Ten miles further south on US 1 and across the bridge spanning the wide mouth of the Kennebec River is the picturesque port city of **Bath**, a thriving community since the early 17th century. This is one locale that is still important in today's shipbuilding industry. Both naval and merchant marine vessels are produced here. You can catch a glimpse of the shipbuilding activity on US 1 as it crosses the Carlton Bridge. Just downstream from the bridge via Washington Street is one of the state's premier attractions – the **Maine Maritime Museum**. The museum complex encompasses several buildings that were former shipbuilding factories in the days of wooden ships. Here, extensive exhibits trace the development of the state's important maritime industry. The site contains a school where apprentices to the boat construction trade are taught (visitors may observe). You can also take boat rides through Bath's busy harbor or board ships that are periodically docked at the museum. A fascinating multi-media exhibit entitled "Lobstering and the Maine

Coast" is one of the best on this other important Maine industry. Children who tire of the more adult-oriented exhibits will love romping in the large outdoor play area. Adults can take a rest on benches while the kids expend some excess energy. Allow at least 90 minutes to visit the Maine Maritime Museum, more if you intend to take a boat ride.

Under 10 miles more on US 1 from Bath will bring you to **Brunswick**, a community of nearly 15,000 people, making it one of the state's larger urban areas. It's also the home of **Bowdoin College**. Take US 1 to Main Street and head south until you reach the attractive 110-acre campus. Besides being host to a number of cultural events such as plays and concerts, Bowdoin contains the College Museum of Art (Walker Building), with its extensive galleries of early American portraits and works by 19th-century European artists. Those less interested in art will probably prefer visiting the Peary-MacMillan Arctic Museum (Hubbard Hall), which chronicles the explorations of the two well known arctic explorers and features exhibits on everyday life in the frozen arctic regions. Allow at least 90 minutes to visit all of the campus' attractions and give yourself a little extra time for strolling about.

A number of old houses in Brunswick also invite your attention. You can see the home of the author of *Uncle Tom's Cabin*, Harriet Beecher Stowe, and that of Joshua Lawrence, a Maine Governor who earned his fame at the Battle of Gettysburg. However, the most lavish of the houses is the **Pejepscot Museum & Skolfield-Whittier House** on Park Row. It's actually two houses and was occupied by two sea captains who built the unusual Italianate structure in the middle of the 19th century. One house is a local history museum, while the other interior has been left untouched from when it was last occupied by the two families in 1925. It's more fascinating than many other old Maine homes and should take at least 45 minutes of your time.

> *Brunswick is a good place for overnight accommodations and for dining.*

US 1 runs into I-95 a couple of miles past town and you can take the latter highway south for eight miles to Exit 20 and the town of **Freeport** as you near the home-stretch back to Portland. But there's a lot to do in and around town. Freeport was the site where Maine was separated from Massachusetts. It's also the original home of

L.L. Bean. Their large headquarters is open 24 hours a day for those of you who get an urge in the middle of the night to buy a sleeping bag. The Bean store has become the center of a large shopping area with more than a hundred stores, the remainder of which stick to more normal operating hours.

Atlantic Seal Cruises leave the wharf in South Freeport on three-hour trips. This excursion makes a stop at Eagle Island State Park, where you can get off and take a look at the Memorial to Robert Peary. It was on Eagle Island where Peary (who had a summer home here) planned his expedition to reach the North Pole. During the fall, Atlantic Seal Cruises offers 2½-hour tours that highlight the coastal foliage.

Use Exit 19 off I-95 to reach two other interesting Freeport attractions. The first is the **Desert of Maine**, two miles west of the exit. Overgrazing here in the early part of this century caused the top layer of soil to erode away, leaving the area a desert. The desert is slowly increasing in size and now covers more than 100 acres, with some dunes reaching almost 70 feet in height. There are 30-minute guided tours of the dunes. A mile south of the Interstate exit via US 1 is the **North American Wildlife Expo**. This beautiful exhibit houses many outstanding dioramas of the animals of North America in their native habitats. Extremely realistic and of interest to all ages, the Expo requires at least 45 minutes to see properly.

From the Wildlife Expo stay on US 1 and head south to **Yarmouth**. The town is only a few miles from Freeport and on Main Street, which crosses US 1, you'll find the **Yarmouth Historical Society and Museum of History**. The name of the place tells you everything you need to know about its contents – all relating to the local area.

You can take either I-95 or US 1 into the nearby town of **Falmouth** and then follow signs to the Maine Audubon Society's **Gilsland Farm**. Located on a more than 60-acre spread of coast by the Presumpscot River, the "farm" includes meadows, woods and tidal marshes. Trails take you through the area, where you will see animals such as muskrats, foxes and many types of birds. There are also a number of exhibits at the Headquarters building. Allow a minimum of 45 minutes.

From Falmouth you can pick up I-295, which will take you the couple of miles back into Portland, where we began our loop journey.

Side Trips and Other Attractions

While the foregoing itinerary takes you through almost every region of Maine and the majority of its most popular sights, there's still more to see if you have the time and inclination. The side trips and other attractions in this section can be done individually or you can do all of them.

If you consult the Maine map at the beginning of this chapter you will notice that the first three side trips all head from the suggested itinerary towards the New Hampshire border and either touch it or come within a few miles. Therefore, if you're going to be combining your Maine trip with a visit to New Hampshire as well, it's almost certain that your connection point between the two states will be via one of these three routes. If so, you'll at least cover one side trip without adding any additional mileage.

Side Trip 1: The Western Lakes Area

Total distance (round-trip from main route): 100 miles
Duration: 7 hours

This trip originates at Gorham. Turn left on SR 25 (westbound) and proceed seven miles to your first stop, **Standish**. The **Marrett House**, on SR 25, was built in the latter part of the 18th century and stayed in the same family for nearly 200 years. The numerous styles of furniture that the family purchased during that period presents a living history of furniture. There's a small garden outside with varying seasonal blooms.

Now take SR 35 north for two miles to the town of **Sebago Lake** and then turn left onto SR 114. This route follows closely along the shore of attractive lake, the second largest in the state, covering almost 46 square miles. It's noted for its excellent fishing opportunities. Sebago is 400 feet deep in some places and is a primary source of water for the city of Portland. At the town of East Sebago, about 10 miles past where you joined the lakeshore, follow SR 107 into Sebago. Here the main attraction is the **Jones Museum of Glass and Ceramics**. More than 8,000 different items are on display, including some works from ancient Egypt. The collection spans the history of man and cultures from every corner of the world. Although you might not think it would take long to look at this collection, you should give yourself a minimum of 45 minutes.

Go back to East Sebago and continue on SR 114 to **Naples**, just to the northwest of the lake. The town was important in the operation of a canal system that connected the region with Portland. A causeway on Long Lake is the departure point for cruises on the *Songo River Queen II*. Boarding an old-fashioned riverboat, you have the option of an hour-long cruise on Long Lake or a 2½-hour excursion along the Songo River. This trip goes through a number of hand-operated locks, some of which have been in use since the 1830s.

From Naples take US 302 west along the shore of Long and Highland Lakes until you reach **Fryeburg**, a mile from the New Hampshire state line. The Saco River is a popular spot for boating and other water-related activities. The town is a good place for a meal before heading back towards the main route.

Side Trip 2: To Grafton Notch and Maine's White Mountains

Total distance (round-trip from main route): 165 miles
Duration: One full day (overnight accommodations, if needed, in Bethel or Rumford)

This trip begins about four miles north of Poland Spring at the intersection of SRs 11 and 26. Take SR 26 north. Your first stop comes after 15 miles at the town of **Paris**. In a converted jail dating from the early 19th century is the **Hamlin Memorial Library**. Hannibal Hamlin is far from a household name in America, but Mr. Hamlin was vice-president under Abraham Lincoln. Many of his belongings are on display, as are other original items depicting local history from the 1800s. Backtrack a few miles to South Paris and take SR 117 towards Buckfield for nine miles to the junction of SR 140. About 13 miles on SR 140 brings you to Canton, where you'll head south on SR 108 for five more miles to **Livermore**. The **Norlands Living History Center** is an actual working farm established in 1870 and covering well over 400 acres. A number of period buildings, all furnished, dot the grounds and there are demonstrations of crafts and food preparation appropriate to that time. Guided tours are given or you can explore the Center on your own. You will need about 90 minutes to cover everything.

Now head back the other way on SR 108 until it joins US 2 at Rumford. Then take US 2 west to Newry (16 miles) at the junction of SR 26 north. This road will take you to beautiful **Grafton Notch State Park**. Although New Hampshire is best known for the White Mountains, the mountains spill over into this section of Maine. The park is traversed by a portion of the Appalachian Trail and contains many peaks well over 3,000 feet. Among the places where you should stop to admire the scenery (all short walks) are two waterfalls (Screw Auger Falls and Mother Walker Falls) and Moose Cave. The Notch also has a number of lovely meadows. Allow about 90 minutes to visit the park. Head back the other way on SR 26 to Newry. This time stay on 26 south for five more miles to Bethel.

Bethel is one of Maine's most popular resorts. Outdoor activities abound in the area's forests, lakes and rivers. Skiing is popular in the winter. Two areas in town, Broad Street and Bethel Hill Village, contain many historic homes. You can just wander around or get a brochure that describes the houses from the local Chamber of Commerce (most are closed to the public, with the notable exception of the **Dr. Moses Mason House** on Broad Street).

Take SR 26 still south from Bethel to **West Paris**, an area rich in minerals and gemstones. **Perham's of West Paris** sells various gems that are mined in the area, and you're free to look around the many displays, especially the separate Maine Mineral Museum with its hundreds of exhibits. The store sells maps that will guide you to one of several area quarries, where you can have free access to hunt for your own gems. Allow about 30 minutes for Perham's and at least double that if you're going to try your hand at hunting for stones. After West Paris, just continue on SR 26 until you return to the main route.

Side Trip 3: The Carrabassett Valley and Rangely Lakes

Total distance (round-trip from main route): 140 miles
Duration: 7 hours (overnight accommodations, if required, in Rangely)

The final side trip in the trio that runs near to New Hampshire starts at Skowhegan. From there, proceed west on US 2 for about 27 miles to the town of Farmington. In an area of pretty rolling hills and many lakes, Farmington is the site of the **Nordica Homestead Museum**, two miles north of town via SR 4. Lillian Nordica was an opera singer of renown. Guided tours of her home are available and exhibit areas contain many of her stage costumes and jewelry, along with numerous trinkets she gathered during her career. Allow 30 minutes.

Continue north on SR 4, an attractive route that mostly parallels the Sandy River until it reaches **Rangely**, 40 miles from your previous stop. **Rangely Lake** is one of many large lakes in the area that make it popular with outdoor enthusiasts. Good fishing, swimming and boating opportunities are available all over, one of the best places being in **Rangely Lakes State Park** on the lake's south shore (you'll pass it later on in your circuit through the area). Several attractions lie a bit past Rangely. The first, three miles west from Rangely on SR 4, is the **Hunter Cove Sanctuary**. Bordering the lake, the sanctuary has trails through forests, cedar swamps and meadows. Allow at least 45 minutes. Only a mile after the sanctuary is the **Wilhelm Reich Museum**. Reich was a psychologist and a disciple of Sigmund Freud. His home's study and library house his art collection and numerous personal artifacts. For children, there is a hands-on "laboratory" to help develop sharper use of the senses. There's also a short nature trail on the grounds. Allow about 30 minutes, unless you're traveling with children who are going to use the lab; in that case, allow another half-hour.

At the end of Rangely Lake turn left onto SR 17, passing the aforementioned State Park, then follow the south shore of the lake back to SR 4. Turn right and proceed to the junction of SR 142 at Phillips. From there it's 15 miles to Kingfield, site of the **Stanley Museum**. A tribute to the pioneering products of the Stanley family (of "Stanley Steamer" fame), the museum houses a large art collection depicting life in rural Maine. There are also four steam-powered automobiles representing the full range of Steamers that were produced by Stanley. Allow 30-45 minutes.

From Kingfield, follow SR 16 for 16 miles to the attractive little town of **North Anson**. In town you'll have a great view of a narrow gorge where the Carrabasset rushes through on its way toward the Kennebec River. Then pick up US 201A on the south side of town and take that back to US 2. Head east for the final five miles back to Skowhegan.

Side Trip 4: Baxter State Park

Total distance (round-trip from main route):
120 miles to/from park entrance.
Duration: See description below.

This trip originates at Howland. Take I-95 north for 28 miles to Exit 56. Then follow SR 11 to Millinocket, then north to Baxter State Park. The trip's total mileage is measured only to the southern entrance of the park, then back to Howland. The park contains only unpaved roads that run for many miles. Your total distance will, therefore, depend upon how much you explore the interior. Baxter is a vast wilderness encompassing more than 200,000 acres. It is crossed by an extensive system of trails ranging from leisurely strolls around ponds and lakes and walks through the forest all the way to a climb of Mt. Katahdin. Boating and fishing are extremely popular activities. There's plenty of wildlife to be seen, including beaver, bear, caribou, deer, and moose. Although the park is developed, it is primarily for those seeking a true wilderness experience. If that doesn't interest you, the trip would be a waste. If this kind of experience does appeal to you, however, this is a paradise where you could spend a day or a week. For further information on Baxter State Park, consult Addendum 3. Return to the main route by reversing the approach route.

Side Trip 5: Aroostook – The North Country

Total distance (round-trip from main route): 365 miles.
Duration: One to two days.
Accommodations in Presque Isle and Caribou.

This rather long journey originates in the same place as Side Trip 4, but reaches the most northern part of Maine where even the summers are always cool. Aroostook is Maine's largest county and is surrounded on three sides by Canada. Mostly a forested area with huge lumbering tracts, it does have several towns of interest scattered primarily along US 1. Everyone living south of Aroostook (even if in Maine) is called a "southerner" to residents of the "north county," as it's fondly called. Aroostook is a beautiful area, tranquil and wide open – just the sort of place that comes to mind when you think of Maine.

From the main route departure point, stay on I-95 until Exit 62 (about 90 miles) and the town of Houlton. Located in **Pierce Park** is a fountain entitled "The Boy with the Leaking Boot." It's from the World War I era and is believed to represent a boy bringing water to injured soldiers. Similar statues from the same period exist in Europe, although the sculptor is unknown.

Houlton lies along US 1 and you'll now proceed north on that route to the town of **Presque Isle**, largest city in Aroostook, with over 10,000 residents. South of town is the **Presque Isle State Park**, loaded with recreational opportunites but now known as the launch site for the trans-Atlantic balloon crossing of the *Double Eagle II* in 1978. A replica of the balloon is on the site. In town, the campus of the University of Maine at Presque Isle is attractive.

About 13 miles north of Presque Isle is **Caribou**, one of the coldest places in the lower 48 states. Lucky for you that you're not coming in winter! It's one of the largest potato farming regions in the country. Among the town's three museums, the **Nylander Museum** is the largest. Many Swedes settled in the area and Olof Nylander was a naturalist who collected various rocks and minerals as well as fossils and Indian artifacts. All of his collections are on display at the Museum, along with items from other sources. The butterfly and mounted bird exhibits are especially interesting.

Allow about 45 minutes. The **Thomas Heritage House** was the home of an early settler in the area and its furnishings reflect the 1880s. The **Caribou Historical Museum** has information on the history of Caribou and its people.

Twenty miles further north on US 1 is **Van Buren**. This was originally a French Canadian settlement and its Acadian heritage is still very much in evidence. The **Acadian Village**, five miles north of town along US 1, contains almost 20 reconstructed buildings including a store, blacksmith shop, church, school and several homes. All are typical of a 19th-century Acadian community. Allow about an hour to see all of the buildings.

After Van Buren, US 1 follows the course of the mighty Saint John River. At the town of Madawaska, directly across the bridge from Edmundston, New Brunswick, you'll be in Maine's most northerly community. Enthusiasts of industrial facilities will certainly enjoy the hour-long guided tours of the **Fraser Paper** mill on Bridge Street.

US 1 continues winding its way along the scenic river to the historic town of **Fort Kent**. This is where US 1 ends, having originated all the way down in Key West, Florida. The **Fort Kent State Historic Site** was built in 1839 during a period of border disputes with Canada. The blockhouse and exhibits describe the events of the era.

From Fort Kent head south on SR 11. The next 50 miles or so are highly scenic as the road snakes alongside rivers and lakes and through heavy forests. Eagle, St. Froid and Portage Lakes are among the largest and most picturesque lakes that you'll encounter. Ten miles before reaching I-95 and the final leg back to the main route, you'll pass through **Patten**. Although small, Patten has always played a vital role in the lumber industry. The **Lumberman's Museum**, a half-mile west of town on SR 159, explores every facet of the industry with thousands of exhibits spread out over nine different buildings. Allow at least one hour. (Note: SR 159 also provides access to Baxter State Park via the north entrance if you wish to combine Side Trips 4 and 5 together.) From Patten, it's less than 70 miles back to this side trip's originating point.

Other Attractions

All of the remaining attractions described in this section are located along Maine's mid-coast region, accessed from US 1. They're close as the crow flies but, because of the coast's many indentations, the mileage adds up. For this reason (and because many of the attractions are similar to those seen on other portions of the main itinerary), we didn't make it a separate side trip or alternative route. Rather than trying to see all of them, we suggest you pick out those of greatest interest. This method won't add a lot of miles to the main itinerary. Attractions are described in order as you travel southbound on US 1 between Damariscotta and Bath.

PEMAQUID POINT (via SR 129 and then SR 130): **Colonial Pemaquid** and **Fort William Henry State Historic Sites** are both on a small peninsula and each dates from the 17th century. The former are the remains of the original fort, with a museum that contains artifacts discovered on the site. Fort William Henry is a reproduction of the original. You can cover both, including the short distance between them, in about an hour. **Lighthouse Park** contains an 1827 lighthouse (closed to the public, but very attractive) and a museum about the fishing industry. There's also a small art gallery.

The adjacent town of **New Harbor** offers the opportunity to sail on the *Hardy III* **Boat Tour**. A variety of trips are offered, ranging from just an hour to more than six hours. Destinations include some of the offshore islands, where seals and puffins can often be seen on the rocky shores.

BOOTHBAY HARBOR (via SR 27): The scenic road to Boothbay Harbor brings you to a charming coastal artists' town. Boat tours of the islands and rivers are also available here. The **Boothbay Railway Village** shows how Maine's towns looked a hundred years ago, with emphasis on the role of the railroads. In addition to seeing the restored buildings and railroad artifacts, you can take a ride on a narrow-gauge steam train. Including the train ride, give yourself at least 90 minutes to tour the village.

GEORGETOWN (via SR 127): The **Josephine Newman Sanctuary** is another facility of the Maine Audubon Society and covers nearly 120 acres of coastal marsh and forest. Teeming with animal life and many varieties of trees, the sanctuary's easy walking trails can provide an hour of interesting nature study.

POPHAM BEACH (via SR 209): Like the other towns in this final section, Popham Beach is on a small peninsula with a rugged and irregular coast. Popham Beach State Park is a popular spot for swimming, while **Fort Popham State Historic Site** features a brick garrison built in the early stages of the Civil War, but never completed. On the same site is a fort of World War II vintage designed to defend against incursions by German submarines. You can climb up on the observation towers or down into the bunkers. Allow 45 minutes to an hour.

New Hampshire

The Granite State

Like its neighbors to the east and west, New Hampshire has much of what people think of when they hear New England mentioned – small but picturesque towns, friendly people, plenty of lakes and rivers, an appreciation of its historic traditions, and a way of life that differs sharply from that of the hectic urban areas further south. According to a major insurance company, New Hampshire is the healthiest state in the nation. It even has its own short stretch of Atlantic coastline for the surf lover. But more than anything else, the Granite State is dominated by the beautiful White Mountains, highest in all of New England, and offering scenic and recreational opportunities of every kind.

The majority of New Hampshire's land is forested and so are its mountains. Although the Green Mountains are in neighboring Vermont, summers in New Hampshire make the name White Mountains something of a misnomer. Sure, the white granite shows through in plenty of places, but the green-covered slopes of the mountains give a refreshing look to them. New Hampshire's mountains and scenic roads are famous for their many "notches," which are called passes or gaps in most other parts of the country.

You'll be pleasantly surprised at how much there is to see in a state that is only 250 miles long and less than 100 miles across at its widest point. But then again, good things come in small packages.

Along the Suggested Itinerary

We'll begin our New Hampshire loop in the city of **Manchester**, the state's largest and the only one with a population approaching six figures. If you're flying to New Hampshire, Manchester is the logical choice. Its newly renovated airport is the busiest in the region and is less than a mile from I-293, which gives easy access to I-93 and all points in the state. For those flying to Boston, just take

I-93 north. It's only 40 miles to the point where it first intersects the suggested itinerary, a little south of Manchester. If you're driving from other parts of the country, there are about a half-dozen major entry points that quickly intersect the tour described in this chapter.

To reach downtown Manchester from I-93, use Exit 6 and take Hanover Street west about two miles. Hanover is the primary east-west road through the center of Manchester, while Elm Street is the main north-south street. Four points of interest are within a short walking distance of one another in the center of town. First is the **Currier Gallery of Art** (on Orange Street). The ornate 1929 structure, built in Italian Renaissance style, houses a collection of European paintings and sculpture spanning six centuries, as well as numerous examples of American arts, crafts and furniture. Allow about an hour to tour the gallery. The **Zimmerman House**, a short ride from here, was designed by Frank Lloyd Wright and is an example of one of his small homes built with practical considerations in mind. The owners also gathered quite an art collection. The house can be visited only on reserved tours that depart by van from the Currier Gallery. Tours last 90 minutes.

Next stop on the agenda is the **Manchester Historic Association** at 129 Amherst Street. The exhibits contain a wide variety of artifacts dealing with local history. Of special note is a collection of documents on the Amoskeag Manufacturing Company. This organization was of great importance during the era when Manchester was a giant in the textile manufacturing business. Allow about three-quarters of an hour.

Two attractions on Concord Street are the **Manchester Institute of Arts and Sciences**, with diverse exhibits covering a number of topics and the **Centre Franco-Americain**. The latter is an unusual exhibit dedicated to the preservation of French heritage in North America.

Not far from downtown and reached via Exit 5 from I-93 and then Bodwell Road is the **Lawrence Lee Scouting Museum**. This contains a huge collection of Boy Scout memorabilia from all over the world. It will be of special interest to anyone who ever spent time in Scouting. Allow between 30 and 45 minutes.

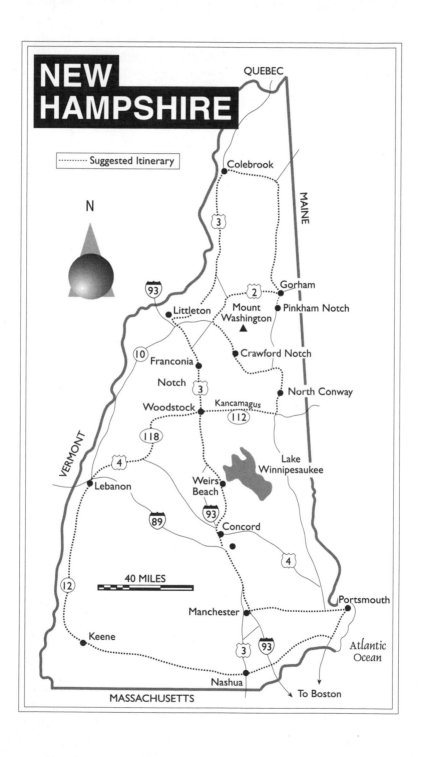

> *Manchester has most of the major nationwide and regional hotel chains and much more cosmopolitan dining than is usually found in the small towns of New England.*

There's a good selection of cultural events, including theater and concerts. For more information on current shows get a copy of the Greater Manchester Visitors Information Guide from the Chamber of Commerce, downtown on Elm Street.

Leave Manchester by SR 101 heading westbound. SR 101 can be reached via Hanover Street from downtown or by taking Exit 7 off I-93 from another direction. It's about 30 miles from Manchester to **Exeter**. A stronghold of anti-Royalist sentiment in the Revolutionary era, Exeter was the temporary capital of New Hampshire. Today it may be better known as home of the respected preparatory school, Phillips Exeter Academy. The historical aspects of Exeter can be appreciated best by visiting the **American Independence Museum** (Governors Lane at Water Street). This structure was at one time the home of New Hampshire's Colonial governor and was built in the early 1720s. The restored home contains some original furniture of Governor Gilman's family, but the more interesting section has copies of the Declaration of Independence, the Constitution and other important documents, as well as an extensive collection of items from the Revolutionary War era. A recreation of a late 18th-century tavern is also in the museum. Allow at least 45 minutes. Both self-guided and guided tours are available. Adjacent to the Museum is the **Gilman Garrison House**. The house was built before 1700 and contains many furniture pieces from both the 17th and 18th centuries. Of most interest, however, is the building itself. Built with heavy logs and gate, the house was essentially a fortress; hence, the name.

From the middle of Exeter pick up SR 101 and take it 12 miles north to one of New England's most historic and interesting cities – **Portsmouth**. The area is also the heart of activities along New Hampshire's short but attractive Atlantic coastline. When the first settlers to Portsmouth arrived, they were lucky enough to find strawberries growing wild. Thus, the name Strawberry Banke was given to the settlement that was to eventually become Portsmouth. A majority of the city's historic homes are in a section called the Strawberry Banke and it's the best place to experience Portsmouth. SR 101 will run into Middle Street as you arrive in town; take that to the junction of US 1, turn left (north) for a quarter of a mile to Route 1B and make a right – you're now in **Strawberry Banke**.

There's no better place to begin your Portsmouth tour than at the large **Strawberry Banke Museum**. This was the site of the original settlement. Today covering 10 acres, the museum has almost 50 buildings spanning about 250 years of Portsmouth's history. Some have been restored to their original condition, while others are still undergoing restoration. Don't expect to find only colonial history on display; the diverse exhibits even include a grocery store that dramatizes life on the home front during the Second World War. Many demonstrations of Revolutionary era crafts take place throughout the day and you can stroll through four different gardens representing different times in the history of Strawberry Banke. Allow at least 90 minutes to appreciate this unique living museum.

Separating the Museum and the riverfront is **Prescott Park**. You can walk along through an attractive garden and visit a museum of folk art containing ship models in a building that once served as a warehouse at the beginning of the 18th century.

Not all of the historic homes are at the Strawberry Banke Museum. While they are scattered throughout the city, many are close to the Banke and are included in a historic tour called the "Portsmouth Trail." You can get a map of the trail at any of the houses on the route. Perhaps of greatest interest is the **John Paul Jones House** (Middle and State Streets and walking distance from the Museum). The structure was built in 1758 and, after a few years, it became a rooming house. The most notable guest was John Paul Jones himself, who resided here in 1777 and again in 1781. Costumed guides offer tours of the house, which is devoted mostly to Jones and artifacts from the early American naval vessels *Ranger* and *America*. Give yourself about 45 minutes to see this house and 30-45 minutes for any of the others in the list that follows: **Langdon House** (early New Hampshire Governor's home and one of the city's finest dwellings); **Rundlet-May House** (early 19th-century merchant's home is a three-story mansion); **Warner House** (dating from the early part of the 18th century and noted for thick brick walls and rich wall panelling, the house has a lightning rod believed to have been put in place by Benjamin Franklin); and the **Wentworth-Gardner House** (Georgian-style structure from the mid-18th century and containing many intricate woodcarvings). Not part of the above grouping of houses but still worth a brief look is the **Jackson**

House (Northwest Street), notable because it is the oldest house in New Hampshire, having been built in 1664.

The **Port of Portsmouth Maritime Museum/Albacore Park** off Market Street is home to *USS Albacore*, a 1950s vintage submarine considered to be the first of the "modern" submarines that replaced those of World War II. Guided tours are given and there's a visitor center that explains more about the vessel. The Park contains a Memory Garden that commemorates those members of the Submarine Service who gave their lives serving their country. It takes about an hour to complete the tour, seeing the visitor center (including film) and gardens.

Two miles from downtown via SR 1A is the **Wentworth-Coolidge Mansion**. Built in the late 1600s, the large home contains over 40 rooms and was the residence of New Hampshire's first Royal Governor. Of interest in this National Historic Landmark is the council chamber, where the state's provisional government carried out its functions during the period immediately before the Revolution. Allow at least a half-hour.

South of town via US 1 and Elwyn Road is the unusual **Urban Forestry Center**. The Center contains marshes, an arboretum and wildflowers with numerous trails and attractive gardens. You can take part in programs that teach about the forest's life-cycle, natural resources and the environment. Allow at least 45 minutes but, since the Center covers nearly 200 acres, you could spend much more time here.

The little kids should see the historical and educational attractions discussed above, but they'll certainly enjoy the **Children's Museum of Portsmouth**, downtown in the South Meeting House on Marcy Street at the edge of Strawberry Banke. The exhibits change frequently, but all involve hands-on activities designed to get you involved in science. **Water Country** provides a different type of diversion. On US 1 three miles south of the city, Water Country contains numerous "get-wet" rides and attractions. Allow several hours, especially in view of the hefty admission prices that these types of attractions get.

No visit to Portsmouth would be complete without a boat ride. One of the most popular is the **Isle of Shoals Steamship Company** leaving from Barker Wharf on Market Street. Sites of historic importance are pointed out, including the naval shipyard, and a stop is made at Star Island, an attractive resort area. Trips last about 2½ hours. Depending on the season, the Steamship Company also offers whale watching and fall foliage cruises. **Portsmouth Harbor Cruises** (Ceres Street Dock) sails on a smaller vessel, the 49-passenger *Heritage*, and tours the harbor as well as cruising around the 14 islands in Portsmouth's harbor. Two cruises are available, one lasting an hour and the other about 2½ hours. The longer cruise also heads inland, sailing up the rivers of the Great Bay.

> *The Portsmouth area has plenty in the way of lodging, dining and shopping. Many of the inns are of a historic nature and are worth taking a look at even if you're not staying there. Among these are the Exeter Inn and the Sheraton Portsmouth Hotel.*

From Portsmouth take SR 1A south over the Sagamore Creek and turn left on SR 1B, following the latter to the nearby suburb of **New Castle**. Two historic attractions are here, the **Fort Constitution Historic Site** and the **Fort Stark Historic Site**. The first is on SR 1B and overlooks Portsmouth Harbor. Only small portions of the original wall remain, but with the information plaques and a little imagination you can get a good picture of what it was like when American colonists captured the fort in December of 1774. Fort Stark is on Wild Rose Lane overlooking the Little Harbor. There are great views from the 10-acre site, which remained an active fort from the middle of the 18th century through World War II. Allow 30-45 minutes for visiting Fort Stark.

Head south on SR 1A and soon you'll reach the town of **Rye**, a very popular seaside resort area. While you might want to take a dip in the ocean at either Jenness State Beach or Wallis Sands State Beach, Rye also is home to the **Odiorne Point State Park**, which houses the **Seacoast Science Center**. The Park is a coastal sanctuary covering more than 300 acres with trails and a visitor information center. The Science Center features natural history exhibits emphasizing marine life. Allow at least an hour for the two attractions.

Cruises also run from Rye. **New Hampshire Seascoast Cruises** (on SR 1A) offers two-hour cruises to the Isle of Shoals, as well as half-day whale watching excursions.

> *Accommodations are available in just about every community along the short New Hampshire coast, including Rye.*

Continuing down the oceanfront you'll soon reach the **Hamptons**, more specifically the towns of North Hampton, Hampton, Hampton Beach and Hampton Falls. All border one another within a small area. Settled in the 1630s, this is home to many attractive state beaches and fishing piers, where you can hop on a chartered fishing boat. The colorful **Fuller Gardens** off SR 1A in North Hampton cover only two acres but include an amazing variety of both perennial and annual flowers.

You might recall that in the 1970s there was a big controversy over nuclear power with the building of the Seabrook Nuclear Generating Station. Things have calmed down a lot and you can visit the **Seabrook Station Science and Nature Center** on SR 1 in the oceanfront community of the same name. The modern visitor center has exhibits on energy and the environment (only the company point of view, please). A nature trail winds its way for three-quarters of a mile through coastal marsh and woodlands. You can also take a very interesting bus tour of the power plant and stop at a training simulator which duplicates the station's control room (maybe then you'll toe the company line). Allow 60-90 minutes if you'll be taking the tour, otherwise half that time will do nicely.

From Seabrook take SR 107 east 14 miles to Kingston and the junction of SR 111. Turn south (left) on the latter and follow it 12 miles to **North Salem**. Follow Haverhill Road for one mile south to **America's Stonehenge**. As the advertisements proclaim, this is a "4,000 year old mystery" – an array of stone structures believed to have been erected by native Americans for astronomical observations or ceremonies. Carbon-dating has verified the approximate age. Give yourself about 45 minutes for a self-guiding tour through the megaliths.

Now follow SR 111 south again until you reach SR 28. Turn left and go three miles to Salem. About a mile west near the junction of I-93 is **Canobie Lake Park**, a large amusement park that will delight the kids and adults too! It has a large number of modern, high-tech thrill rides among the 75-odd attractions, but Canobie Lake Park is older than most. Accordingly, you'll find an old-time carousel (authentic hand-carved horses from the 19th century), a paddlewheel riverboat and a narrow-gauge steam train. There are also numerous shows where you can relax after you've come off the wild roller coasters, log flumes and so forth. The time you spend here depends on your ability to handle the rides, but plan on staying a minimum of three hours and perhaps twice that.

Now resume your westward journey on SR 111 and in 12 miles you'll reach **Nashua**, one of New Hampshire's largest cities and located right on the Massachusetts border. Nashua is an important industrial and commercial center. Two historic attractions are located in the center of town. These are the **Abbot-Spalding House Museum** (Nashville Street) and the adjacent **Florence Hyde Speare Memorial Building**. The former is a restored federal-style home. The Speare Memorial has several art galleries and local history exhibits.

From central Nashua follow SR 101A to the Everett Turnpike. Take the Turnpike north to Exit 10 in the adjacent community of **Merrimack** and follow your eyes and nose to the New Hampshire home of **Anheuser-Busch** on US 3 (Daniel Webster Highway). A comprehensive tour of the brewery explains the entire process of beermaking, all the way up to packaging. A highlight is a visit to the stables, where one of the company's famous teams of Clydesdale horses are kept. Other notable points of interest at Anheuser-Busch are the very attractively landscaped grounds and "The Hamlet," a group of European-style buildings complete with gift shop. Tours end at the hospitality room, where you can sample Bud and other products. Children are served soft drinks. Allow at least an hour for this attraction, which is one of the state's most popular.

> *There are plenty of places to eat and stay in the Nashua-Merrimack region, mostly at exits off the Everett Turnpike, a toll road, and along US 3.*

Just north of the brewery, US 3 crosses Amherst Road. Turn left and follow this road for five miles to Amherst. Then pick up SR 101 westbound and take it for 12 miles to Wilton at the junction of SR 31. By now you've made the transition from the low-lying coastal region to the beginnings of New Hampshire's mountains, although they rarely exceed 2,000 feet in this area. North of town via SR 31 is **Frye's Measure Mill**, a mid-18th-century textile mill that still uses very early equipment for producing wool garments. There are tours of the mill and demonstrations. The tours take about 90 minutes, perhaps too long and detailed for most people.

Whether or not you opt to visit the mill, continue west on SR 101 (backtrack from SR 31 if you did go to the mill). In about eight miles you'll reach a signed cutoff for **Miller State Park**. The Park features a short scenic drive to the summit of Pack Monadnock Mountain. The almost 2,300-foot peak can also be reached by trail. Allow about a half-hour if going by car and a minimum of 90 minutes if you're going to be adventurous and make the ascent on foot. It's not difficult, but it is time consuming.

Return to SR 101 and continue west, where you'll soon reach the historic town of **Peterborough**, now an important art colony. The **Peterborough Historical Society and Museum** (Grove Street) comprises a museum building with exhibits on local history and several old homes. Allow 30-45 minutes. The **Shieling State Forest**, northwest of town, is a 45-acre preserve with more than two miles of trails. The Forestry Learning Center strives to teach visitors about forestry management. Allow at least a half-hour.

Now return to SR 101, heading west one last time for the 20-mile ride to **Keene**. Dating from the late 18th century, it is now the home of **Keene State College**, where plays and other cultural events are frequently staged.

> *Nice accommodations and dining can be found in Keene.*

Shopping is made more interesting at the **Colony Mill Marketplace**, a restored wool mill. Located on West Street, off Main, it now contains 35 stores and restaurants. There's free entertainment periodically. Main Street is also the site of two other attractions, both within walking distance from the Colony Mill. First is the **Horatio Colony Museum**, dating from 1806. It was built by one of the area's first settlers and was later owned by a prominent Keene family. One such owner (with the unusual last name of Colony) was a world traveler and gathered a large collection of unusual items, now on display in the house. The **Wyman Tavern Museum** was both a home and an inn and was built in 1762. It has a long and storied past from the Revolutionary era and was the first meeting place of the trustees of Dartmouth University.

Main Street is SR 12. Follow it north when leaving Keene. In 14 miles you'll reach the Connecticut River, where the road turns and heads due north. The river forms an attractive boundary between New Hampshire and Vermont. Stay along the river and SR 12 for approximately 16 miles until you reach the town of **Charlestown**. This small town has one of New Hampshire's largest historic districts. The **Charlestown Historic District** along Main Street encompasses more than 45 structures dating from the 18th century. You can pick up a descriptive booklet at any of the open buildings along the route. Located at a large Colonial estate right on Main Street is the **Foundation for Biblical Research**. While the less-than-pious may not be interested in the various Bible-study programs, just about everyone will find enjoyment in the collection of artifacts found during archaeological expeditions in the Holy Land.

Near the river just east of town on SR 11 is the unusually named **Fort at Number Four Living History Museum**. The reconstruction depicts the original Charlestown settlement of 1744-1746, which was abandoned due to raids by Indians. Twelve buildings have been recreated, including the stockade. Period furnishings and demonstrations lend authenticity to the site, which is worth at least 45 minutes of your time.

State Routes 11 and 12 are contiguous with one another as you head north from Charlestown for a dozen miles to your next destination, **Claremont**. This historic community is centered around Tremont Square, where you'll find nearly 40 early buildings still in use. You can visit these on a walking tour. The **Claremont Society Museum** (Mulberry Street) contains New England memorabilia with an emphasis on local history. Finally, the 800-seat **Opera House** was built in 1897 and is on the National Register of Historic Places. The building is worth a brief look, but if you're interested in attending a performance, inquire at the box office.

After Claremont stay on SR 12 into SR 12A and continue north along the Connecticut River. Five miles north on SR 12A is a covered wooden bridge dating from 1866. While New Hampshire still maintains many of these relics of a bygone era, this particular structure is one of the longest in the country, measuring 460 feet.

Proceed about two miles past the bridge and into **Cornish**. Immediately north of town is the **Saint-Gaudens National Historic Site**. This was the home and studio of the well known Irish sculptor, who created many large figures for various public monuments throughout the country. The home was originally a tavern from the very early 19th century. Today, you can tour his home and two studios. The home contains his original furnishings, while the studios display many of his tools and works. Also on the grounds are trails through the woods and a pleasant and colorful formal garden. Give yourself at least 1¼ hours for the visit.

From Cornish it's an additional 18 miles north via SRs 12 and then 10 to the attractive village of Hanover. The town's claim to fame is as the home of **Dartmouth College,** dating from 1769 and one of the most prestigious of the Ivy League schools (meaning, of course, great academics and lousy football). Some of the campus buildings date from the late 18th century, but a stroll along Dartmouth Row and other portions of the grounds will reveal a diversity of architectural styles that somehow maintain a harmonious appearance. Among the buildings you should see on your 45-60-minute visit are the Baker Library, containing nearly two million volumes and impressive murals portraying the history of North America, the Hood Museum of Art and the Webster Cottage, which was for a time the residence of Daniel Webster. There are many cultural performances at the Hopkins Center.

From Hanover take SR 120 south six miles into **Lebanon.**

> *There's a good choice of lodging and dining in Lebanon, better than in Hanover.*

Pick up I-89 south for two miles to Exit 17 and then go east on US 4 to the town of **Enfield.** Founded in the 1780s, Enfield has a population of about 4,000. It was originally a Shaker religious community and was active as such until 1923. The **Museum at Lower Shaker Village** (south of town via 4A) will acquaint you with the beliefs and lifestyles of the Shakers. As there are many buildings and craft demonstrations to view, give yourself at least an hour. Also of interest in Enfield is the **LaSalette Shrine,** a replica of the Shrine of the Blessed Virgin Mary in LaSalette, France. The very attractive grounds contain a Rosary Pond and chapel, colorful gardens and a "Peace Walk." There's also a walk through the Stations of the Cross. Give yourself about a half-hour at LaSalette. If you happen to be in the area on a Saturday night you're in luck because the grounds are beautifully illuminated.

Ten miles east of Enfield along US 4 is **Canaan**. Like so many other communities in the area, Canaan boasts a historic district and a local history museum. The main attraction in the area requires that you detour for eight miles from town (still along US 4 east) to the tiny town of Grafton. Here you'll visit **Ruggles Mine**, first opened in 1803. It consists of a large open pit with several cave-like rooms within its rocky walls and tunnels. You may find some of the more than 150 different types of minerals and you're free to take with you whatever you collect. There's also a collection of minerals on display in the visitor center. Ruggles Mine is an interesting attraction and, in its own weird sort of way, can even be considered beautiful. Allow about 45 minutes.

Return to Canaan and take SR 118 north. From here on in the route will be very scenic as you're about to enter the domain of the White Mountains, even though the famous White Mountain National Forest doesn't begin for another 15 miles. The total distance from Canaan to North Woodstock is about 40 miles, of which the last three are via SR 112. But we're getting a bit ahead of ourselves, so let's backtrack for just a moment. At the junction of SRs 118 and 112, turn left on SR 112 and ride for four miles to the first of many White Mountain attractions, the **Lost River** in beautiful Kinsman Notch.

The Lost River was formed eons ago by glaciers. The results of this action include many small caves and "potholes." The river runs through a narrow gorge, sometimes disappearing from view under rocks and ending in a waterfall at the end of the gorge. While the potholes are often up to 60 feet deep, some of the caves are very narrow and you have to squeeze through them. Fortunately, for the hefty among us, you can choose to bypass some or all of the caves and stay on the boardwalks that wind through the gorge. Some of the fanciful names given to formations are the Lemmon Squeezer and Guillotine Rock. There's also a nature trail with hundreds of species of flowers identified. The walk covers about three-quarters of a mile, whether you opt to go through or around any of the caves. Allow about an hour for this unusual work of nature.

After finding your way through the Lost River take SR 112 into **North Woodstock**, one of several towns in the heart of the White Mountains.

> *You'll find plenty of hotels in North Woodstock,*
> *as well as in the neighboring towns of Woodstock*
> *and Lincoln. Dozens of restaurants of all types*
> *can also be found, but the emphasis is on whole-*
> *some and inexpensive family-type dining.*

The next several days of the suggested itinerary will be a series of loops through all of New Hampshire's White Mountains, sometimes within the National Forest borders, but with many attractions located on private and state lands in the area's many scenic notches.

Besides its picturesque location, North Woodstock's main attraction is **Clark's Trading Post**, where you can spend at least 90 minutes on various rides, including the White Mountain Central Railroad. A museum features early cameras and other equipment, as well as some antique fire apparatus. You can even see performing bears.

The White Mountain National Forest covers 800,000 acres (an area slightly larger than Rhode Island) and contains the largest alpine area in the United States east of the Rocky Mountains.

From North Woodstock our White Mountain excursion continues along SR 112, the next 37 miles of which are known as the Kancamagus Highway. But first, in Lincoln, by the Interstate is the **Hobo Railroad**. One-hour trips take visitors alongside the Pemigewasset River and point out places of historic interest. There's also some fun for the kids at the **Whale's Tale Water Park**, another get-wet ride extravaganza where you could spend a lot of time (and money).

The **Kancamagus Highway**, a National Forest highlight, is one of the state's most scenic and unspoiled routes. Although all of the states in this guide have designated various routes as "scenic," the Kancamagus Highway is the only one in New England that has earned the distinction of being a National Scenic Byway. The route goes through the National Forest from Lincoln to Conway in a tranquil valley alongside the Swift River. The highest point on the road is Kancamagus Pass at 2,860 feet. You needn't be worried if you're not an experienced mountain driver, for the route is easy and well maintained. Gentle grades and long turns allow you to appreciate the scenery without working up a sweat. Give yourself about three hours for crossing the route, but be ready to adjust that figure depending upon how many attractions you stop at. Now we'll look at some of the good stopping points along the Kancamagus, in the order you would reach them driving from Lincoln to Conway. There are also several overlooks along the route that are well marked and are worth brief stops.

First is **Loon Mountain**, where you can ride a gondola up to Loon Mountain Park. The ride covers almost a mile and a half to the summit and provides an incredible panorama of the White Mountain National Forest. There's an observation tower at the top, along with various exhibits and recreational opportunities. Shortly after Loon Mountain is attractive **Sabbaday Falls**, which can be reached from the parking area by an easy trail through the woods (round-trip 20 to 30 minutes). Located close to one another are the **Rocky Gorge** and **Lower Falls Scenic Areas**. Just steps away from the road you can stroll along the Swift River as it tumbles over boulders of all shapes and sizes strewn along the course of the river. You can make it a short hike or take a seat on one of the rocks and contemplate the sound of water rushing by as you take in the surrounding mountain and forest scenery.

You'll already know why you came to New Hampshire as you reach the end of the Kancamagus Highway in Conway at the junction of SR 16. Turn left and head north until SR 16 runs into US 302 and the town of North Conway. Many stores, including well-known factory outlets, line Main Street.

> *North Conway is another of many White Mountain communities where lodging and dining can be found in abundance.*

One of the many things to do in the area is to take an hour-long ride on the **Conway Scenic Railroad** (on SR 16/US 302). The railroad and some of the rolling stock still used to transport visitors dates from the 1870s. The 11-mile one-way journey takes you along the Saco River and affords some beautiful White Mountain vistas. Of even greater scenic merit than the train ride in North Conway, however, is a visit to **Echo Lake State Park**, less than two miles off US 302. Although it only covers 400 acres, Echo Lake has an abundance of beauty. First, take a short ride to the top of 700-foot-high Cathedral Ledge for a view of both the mountains and the Saco River Valley. The view of Cathedral Ledge as you approach the park is also beautiful. Echo Lake itself is a stunning sight and is made even more so by the backdrop – another rocky ledge, this one called White Horse Ledge. Allow a minimum of a half-hour.

About 10 miles north of Echo Lake along US 302 (which until Glen is also SR 16) is the town of **Glen**. This Mount Washington Valley community has many attractions, ranging from children's fare to one of the state's best museums. There's also the **Grand Manor Car Museum**, which contains vehicles from the early part of the century. **Storyland** is a delightful wonderland if you have small children, but probably not worth a stop if there are only adults in your party. There are dozens of rides and attractions, most of which are based on popular fairytales, but there are several educational features as well, such as the "Tales of Wonder" theater and "A Child's Visit to Other Lands." Children could spend almost an entire day here, but allow at least three hours.

Finally, **Heritage-New Hampshire** is an outstanding educational experience for people of all ages. The "plot" is a journey through the history of New Hampshire, beginning with your arrival in 1634 on a wooden sailing ship right through to the present. Housed in an impressive large white colonial-style structure, Heritage-New Hampshire uses various multi-media and high-tech methods to document the state's history. The result is a diverse and interesting museum experience. This time machine requires at least 90 minutes.

Just a couple of miles north of Glen on SR 16 is the popular resort community of **Jackson**. It's one of the state's best skiing areas during the winter but is worth visiting in summer for its scenery alone. **Nestlenook Farm** (which is also a hotel) is an interesting attraction (authentic sleigh rides and ice-skating in winter). Beautiful gardens grace the grounds in summer and you can take horseback rides into the surrounding mountains and along meandering rivers.

Return to Glen and continue west on US 302. You're entering Crawford Notch, one of the most scenic of all New Hampshire notches. At Bartlett (seven miles past Glen) is the **Attitash Alpine Slide**, which offers visitors several ways to appreciate the scenery. The most leisurely is by taking a chairlift (there's an observation tower at the top), but the more adventurous can ride on a three-quarter-mile slide. If you keep your eyes open during the drop you can admire the view. Pony rides, trails and some water slides add to the recreational opportunities. Allow about 45 minutes for the chairlift and longer if you're going to be sliding, wet or dry.

US 302 will now wind its way through the notch and, after the appropriately named tiny town of Notchland, enter beautiful **Crawford Notch State Park**. The road through the park adjoins the Saco River as it travels through the deep gorge cut by a vast ice sheet. Views of the Presidential Range are common. Near the northern end of the park are short trails that lead to the Silver and Flume Cascades. The Cascades are almost like a horizontal waterfall – the water runs over gradually sloping rock ledges before finally dropping out of sight as it tumbles down from Mount Webster. A more difficult trail (about two miles round-trip and steep in some places) is the route to Arethusa Falls, one of New Hampshire's highest. The Falls plummet about 200 feet. Allow about 45 minutes for the State Park, but at least double that if you're going to be taking the trip to Arethusa Falls.

As you emerge from Crawford Notch State Park, watch for signs indicating a side road that leads to the base of Mount Washington and the famous **Mount Washington Cog Railway**. You can also ride by car to the top, but that's from the other side of the mountain and we will discuss that below. This is a three-hour round-trip on one of the steepest cog railways in the world. The destination is the 6,288-foot summit of Mount Washington, where the vistas can be magnificent. We say "can" because, unfortunately, Mount Washington has a habit of creating its own weather, and many times it's not good. You may want to inquire about conditions at the top before making the trip. On a clear day you can see several states, Canada and the Atlantic Ocean. While at the top, be sure to stop in at the Sherman Adams Summit Building. In addition to a glass-enclosed observation area, there are interesting exhibits on Mt. Washington's unique environment and human habitation on the mountain. The old steam engines that make the climb use a ton of coal and a thousand gallons of water on each trip. Exhibits at the base station include the engine that made the first climb of Mt. Washington.

Descend from the base station and go back to US 302 heading west towards Twin Mountain. The two communities of Bretton Woods and Twin Mountains have lodging and dining. Speaking of lodging, it's worth stopping in for a brief visit at the **Mount Washington Hotel and Resort**, actually several different facilities and five restaurants. Located on US 302, the elegant Grand Hotel features a

900-foot-long veranda that wraps around the building. From this impressive vantage point you can take in wonderful views of the Presidential Range.

At Twin Mountain, turn right onto SR 115 and proceed 14 miles to the junction of US 2, turning west there towards **Jefferson**. Here are two major attractions, both of which appeal to youngsters. First is **Six Gun City,** where the old west still comes to life each day. There are shows and bank robberies (children can be part of the posse), miniature horses, rides and more. Three dozen buildings recreate a western town and there's a museum with a large collection of carriages and sleighs. A few miles from the old west is **Santa's Village**. Here the theme is mostly Christmas and kids can visit Santa all year round. As at Six Gun City, you can see many shows and go on rides, but Santa's Village also has the "Skyway Sleigh" – a monorail traversing the park. Each of these two attractions requires several hours, so you may have to give some consideration to the best way of allocating your time. Unlike the Kancamagus Highway and the state parks in the notches, this is the commercial side of the White Mountains.

Now head east on US 2 to the town of Gorham, about a half-hour's drive. Turn south on SR 16 and you'll be entering nature once again. This time it's **Pinkham Notch**. Within the notch are such scenic highlights as the Glen Ellis Falls and Crystal Cascades, both reached by short trails. There are also longer trails leading to many other picturesque places. You can get to the top of the notch by taking the **Wildcat Mountain Gondola Tramway**. A trip to the top of the 4,397-foot mountain offers great vistas of Mt. Washington as well as many other peaks in the Presidential Range. Allow at least 45 minutes for the round-trip via the Gondola and about an equal amount of time for Pinkham Notch's other features.

Just north of the Gondola and the lower portion of the notch is the beginning of the **Mount Washington Auto Road**. This leads to the same point at the summit which you reach on the Cog Railway. The road is unpaved and there are very steep grades and hairpin turns. It is definitely *not* for the novice or timid driver. You can have experienced guides drive you in a van. That saves the wear and tear on you and your car, but they won't stop at many of the viewpoints on the way up. Also, there is an exhilarating sense of accomplishment to having climbed Mt. Washington in your own car. Allow at least two hours if you're going to be driving your own vehicle, but don't do it in bad weather. The guided tours take about 90 minutes. Round-trip is approximately 16 miles.

Retrace your route back to Gorham, head west on US 2 for one mile and take SR 16 north for six miles to **Berlin**.

> *Accommodations and dining are plentiful in Berlin and even more so back in Gorham.*

About four miles north of town on a marked spur road is **Nansen Wayside Park**. A 170-foot steel frame ski jump located by a quiet riverbank here is worth a brief look.

Another 26 miles further north on SR 16 will bring you to the junction of SR 26, where you should turn left. This road winds through the northernmost of New Hampshire's notches – **Dixville Notch** – much of which is set aside as a State Park. The scenery here is more rugged than in most of the other notches you've been to thus far and is quite rewarding. Among the most worthwhile of the Notch's sights are the Cascades, unusual rock formations such as the Cathedral Spires and Table Rock (this one accessible via a fairly long trail) and beautiful Gloriette Lake. The latter is best seen from the attractive grounds of the Balsams Resort complex. Allow about two hours for traversing Dixville Notch and seeing its sights, with another hour tacked on if you hike to Table Rock. The Balsams, by the way, is a 15,000-acre complex of timeless architecture and superbly manicured grounds in a splendid natural setting. Like the Mount Washington Hotel and Resort, you make time to look at it even if you don't stay there overnight.

At the western end of Dixville Notch is the town of **Colebrook**, where you can visit the **Shrine of Our Lady of Grace**, a peaceful 25-acre landscaped area studded with many monuments of marble and granite. Give yourself about 30 minutes to walk around and reflect.

Now head south on US 3 for approximately 35 miles to **Lancaster**, oldest community in the northern part of the state. Two miles south of town, still via US 3, is the **Weeks State Park**. Located atop Mount Prospect, the estate at the summit was once the home of John W. Weeks, a cabinet member under two presidents and a United States congressman. It was Mr. Weeks who was responsible for much of the legislation that created the east's National Forests, including the White Mountain National Forest. A visit to the estate will fill you in on the details of his career and you can get an excellent view of the Presidential Range and Vermont's White Mountains from the top of a stone observation tower. The grounds also contain a short nature trail. Allow 30-45 minutes for your visit.

Continue your journey south on US 3 for another 20 miles or so to **Littleton**.

> *A wide range of places to stay can be found in the Littleton-Bethlehem area.*

Littleton has quite a few historic homes, but the primary attraction is eight miles west of town via SR 18. That's the **Moore Station and Dam** on the Connecticut River. The hydroelectric facility provides good views of the river and surrounding mountains and has exhibits on the dam.

From Moore Station pick up I-93 and head south for a short distance to Exit 38 in the town of **Franconia**. Then take SR 116 to the **Frost Place**, the home of the famous poet, Robert Frost. From 1915. he lived in this mid-19th-century farmhouse. The house contains many items relating to the poet, including several signed first editions of his works. A nature trail is sign-posted with his works as well. For those of you who like poetry, a poet is in residence during the summer and gives readings in the barn. Allow 30-45 minutes.

Head south once again on I-93, but only for a few miles to Exit 35. This marks the entrance to **Franconia Notch** and **Franconia Notch State Park**. The deep glacial notch, framed by the high peaks of both the Kinsman and Franconia ranges of the White Mountains, constitutes the best known of New Hampshire's many notches. It may also well be the most beautiful; certainly it contains an abundance of unusual sights. The Notch extends from this point near Exit 35 down to North Woodstock, about 11 miles. The entire length is traversed by I-93 and US 3, known as the Franconia Notch Parkway. Both provide easy access to all of the area's attractions. For simplicity, though, stay on the Parkway, whose slower speeds will allow you to appreciate the passing scenery. The attractions described below are listed in north-to-south order. Rather than allocating time for each feature, simply plan on spending a day to see the Notch.

Echo Lake (not to be confused with Echo Lake State Park near North Conway) is so called because of the natural acoustic affect of the lake's setting, hemmed in on three sides by mountains. This beautiful lake is the largest of several in the Notch. The rock formation known as Artist's Bluff serves as a backdrop. It is reached by a short trail from the roadside parking area.

Next stop on the agenda is the **Cannon Mountain Aerial Tramway II**. Two 80-passenger cable cars make a five-minute journey, from the valley station to the top of 4,180-foot Cannon Mountain, a climb of over 2,000 feet. The total distance traveled to make that vertical ascent is more than a mile. From the summit station there is a grand view of the surrounding mountains and their accompanying valleys. There probably is no other panorama like it in New England. In fact, the Cannon Mountain Tramway experience is simply the best of its type in the eastern United States. The view from the observation deck at the summit station alone is worth the trip but, to enhance it even more, try striking out on one of the several trails leading from the summit. At the base station is the **New England Ski Museum**. It provides an interesting historical perspective of the sport in both the nordic and alpine forms.

The **Old Man of the Mountain** (also known as Great Stone Face or The Profile) is a symbol of New Hampshire and one of its most cherished attractions. The granite rock protrudes from a sheer cliff almost 1,200 feet above Profile Lake, another of the Notch's gems. Many people are surprised to hear that the face of the Old Man of the Mountain has not been carved like Mt. Rushmore, but is a natural phenomenon resulting from the random formation of five separate rock ledges. The distance from the Old Man's chin to his forehead is about 40 feet.

A little further south into the Notch is **The Basin**, a very deep glacial pothole measuring about 20 feet in diameter. It's reached by a short trail from the parking area (you can just about see The Basin when you get out of your car). The sides of the pothole have been worn so smooth by water and debris that they appear to have been polished.

The final attraction needn't take a back seat to anything else in the Notch. **The Flume** is an 800-foot-long narrow gorge at the base of Mt. Liberty. The solid granite walls rise from heights of between 70 and 90 feet and are only 10-12 feet apart. The result is a dark and forbidding vista, almost cave-like, but beautiful at the same time.

The walls, despite the fact that sunlight penetrating the gorge is limited, are thick with moss because of the constant moisture. The gorge contains a stream running through it and several waterfalls. An easy boardwalk provides access through the gorge, although there are stairs and a few steep climbs that may make it difficult for the physically impaired. Buses take visitors from the entrance station and visitor center to a point near the gorge. The rest is on foot. After traversing the gorge, a long trail above it heads back to your point of origination. Along the way are several pools, more waterfalls and plenty of flora. There are even two covered bridges along the walk. The Flume is a delightful experience.

Upon leaving the southern end of Franconia Notch, pick up I-93 southbound and take it to Exit 26 at the town of Plymouth. Then head five miles west on SR 25 to another natural attraction, the **Polar Ice Caves**. Easy paths go through a series of caves and passages filled with boulders and minerals. There's also a glacial rock garden and nature trail. Children will enjoy feeding some of the tame animals in residence. Give yourself about an hour here.

Next return to I-93 south and take it to Exit 24. Drive south on US 3/SR 25 to the town of **Holderness**, which marks the end of the White Mountain area and the beginning of New Hampshire's stunning Lake Region (although the mountains are still clearly visible, especially to the north of the lakes). Holderness is home to the **Science Center of New Hampshire**, a nature center devoted to informing visitors about the animals and plants of the state. The 200-acre sanctuary contains a three-quarter-mile trail that leads past enclosures where the animals live in their natural habitat. There are several buildings along the trail with exhibits and interactive activities to further enhance your understanding of the animals. Allow at least an hour to tour the Center.

Another popular activity in Holderness is a boat ride on **Squam Lake**. Squam Lake Tours and The Original Golden Pond Tours both offer trips of about three hours on this lovely lake. Both visit Church Island, where you can tour the outdoor chapel. The Purgatory Cove section of the lake is where the movie *On Golden Pond* was filmed, thus the name of the second tour operator.

From Holderness, continue south on US 3 for 18 miles to the town of **Weirs Beach**.

> *Accommodations are plentiful in Weirs Beach
> and in the neighboring town of Laconia.*

Weirs Beach lies on Lake Winnipesaukee, the state's largest. The lake contains many islands and, because of the numerous indentations and coves, the shoreline stretches for nearly 300 miles. The best way to see the lake is by taking a boat ride on the 1,350-passenger *MS Mt. Washington*. There is a choice of trips lasting from 2¼ to 3¼ hours. If you're pressed for time, you can take a two-hour trip on a smaller ship. Both depart from the main dock in Weirs Beach. The town itself has the flavor of an amusement park. The main street is filled with arcades and other diversions that stay open well into the night. **Laconia** is a few miles south of Weirs Beach via US 3 and along a series of lakes. Like Weirs Beach, it's a major resort area and recreational opportunities abound.

We'll proceed, however, another seven miles south on US 3 to **Franklin**. This is home to the **Daniel Webster Birthplace** (south of town via US 3 and off SR 127). It won't take long to tour the small two-room structure dating from the mid-1700s, but it's an interesting little piece of Americana.

Now pick up I-93 and take it 10 miles to Exit 18 (Canterbury Center). Follow signs to the **Canterbury Shaker Village**, another of the many such communities established by the Shaker sect, beginning in the latter part of the 18th century. This large complex contains 24 historic buildings, all furnished in authentic Shaker style. Many craft demonstrations are given. You can also see how the Shakers irrigated their farms from ponds they developed and take a stroll along a trail that weaves through herb gardens. Allow 1¼-1½ hours.

Returning to I-93, it's only about 10 more miles to the state capital of **Concord** and, with 36,000 people, one of the largest communities in New Hampshire. Concord is an attractive little city that mixes industry and government well. The Merrimack River winds gracefully through town, separating it into two distinct sections, with the city center lying on the west bank.

Two attractions are in the northern portion of town on your way into the city. Take Exit 16 off I-93, follow SR 132 to Portsmouth Street and you will reach the **Conservation Center**, a facility run by the Society for the Protection of New Hampshire Forests. The

Center features exhibits on the use of passive solar energy, as well as methods of wood heating. In addition, there is a two-mile nature trail that contains just about every variety of flora found in the state. Allow an hour to see all of the exhibits and walk the entire trail.

Now head back to I-93 and take it one exit south to I-393. Use Exit 1 off I-393 and proceed via Institute Drive to the **Christa McAuliffe Planetarium**. This science center is dedicated to the memory of the New Hampshire school teacher who was killed in the *Challenger* space shuttle disaster. The strikingly modern building is a light-reflecting glass pyramid and inside is one of the best planetarium shows around. It lasts about an hour. There are also a number of interactive exhibits.

Access to downtown Concord is via I-93 to Exit 14 and then west on Center Street to Main Street. The remainder of the attractions are located on or near Main. The New Hampshire **State House** (N. Main) is the oldest state capitol in continuous use, having been constructed in 1819. The neoclassic-style structure is built of local granite and Vermont marble. The attractive plaza which has the State House as its central feature also has numerous statues and historical markers, with a Memorial Arch in honor of the state's servicemen and women. Inside the building are 180 portraits of famous New Hampshire personages, as well as the Hall of Flags and four beautiful murals on the walls of the Senate Chamber. There's also a separate visitor center with various exhibits on the state. You can take either guided or self-guided tours. Allow a minimum of 45 minutes.

At Eagle Square, a stone's throw from the capitol, is the **Museum of New Hampshire History**. Relocated to its new larger home in 1995, the building is a renovated 19th-century warehouse. The many galleries and exhibits span five centuries of New Hampshire history and require 45-60 minutes of your time. Back on North Main is the **Kimbal Jenkins Estate**, a Victorian Gothic mansion that dates from around 1880 and was built by a prominent local family. This fine old home is noted for its high ceilings and fancy woodworking. Outside are formal gardens and a children's play area. You can take an hour-long guided tour or see the place on your own, probably in about half that time. This house is among the 17 historic sites on a walking tour called the **Coach and Eagle Trail**. All of the buildings are downtown and you can get a map and descriptive brochure from the Chamber of Commerce at 244 Main, a block from the Kimbal Jenkins home.

The final attraction in this area is the **Pierce Manse** (on Penacock Street), the 1840s home of President Franklin Pierce. The home contains family furnishings and memorabilia of Pierce's presidency. Allow about a half-hour.

> *Concord has reasonably priced lodging and a good choice of restaurants. Several nice eateries are located in historic buildings in the Eagle Square area.*

From Concord back to Manchester is a drive of only 16 miles via I-93. This brings us back to the starting point of the loop and the end of the suggested itinerary. If you flew into Boston, you can return to that city by simply continuing on I-93.

Other Attractions

The suggested itinerary covered the length and breadth of the state and, if you followed it, you qualify as a veteran New Hampshire sightseer. But there is more to see. None of the attractions in this section lies more than 30 miles (one way) from the main route. To make things easier we've grouped them by area. The regions are: The Great Bay; Southern Frontier; Sunapee; White Mountains; and Lakes. Within each area the listings are alphabetic by town.

The Great Bay Area

Northwest of Portsmouth

DOVER (via US 4 and the Spaulding Turnpike from Portsmouth): The **Woodman Institute** consists of three buildings, the Woodman House (1818), Dame Garrison House (1675), and the Hale House (1813). The main emphasis is on period furnishings, but there's also an exhibit on natural history. Allow about 45 minutes.

DURHAM (via US 4 and SR 108): The **Great Bay National Estuarine Research Reserve** covers nearly 5,000 acres of tidal areas and nearly 50 miles of shoreline on this inland bay. Although not highly developed for visitation, there are some exhibits at the headquarters and the bay area is very attractive.

The Southern Frontier

*Between Nashua and Keene south of SR 101,
which connects these two towns*

FITZWILLIAM (via US 202 and SR 119): A typical New England town complete with a village green. The **Rhododendron State Park** here contains some of the largest and hardiest varieties of this beautiful flowering plant in the northern latitudes. Some of the bushes exceed 20 feet in height and the color is a wonderful sight when they're in full bloom during the first half of July. The glen is encircled by a one-mile trail and, in addition to the flowers, you'll get some excellent views of the Monadnock Mountains. Allow about 45 minutes.

JAFFREY (via US 202): A small local museum is housed in an 1833 schoolhouse in **Jaffrey Historic Distric-Melville Academy Museum**. Of more general interest is the **Monadnock State Park,** with a 3,165-foot peak and many miles of trails. There's a visitor center. This happens to be one of the most climbed mountains in the world. Your visit will be short, however, unless you're planning a hike to the top, in which case you should allow several hours. Another way of getting a good view is to take a scenic airplane ride over the Monadnock region at the **Silver Ranch Airpark**. Flights last under an hour. There are also carriage rides for those who wish to stay on the ground.

NEW IPSWICH (via SR 123): The attraction here is the **Barret House**, also known as Forest Hall. An unusual combination of Federal and Gothic architecture, the house was built at the turn of the 19th century. Guided tours are given or you can explore on your own. Allow a minimum of a half-hour and be sure to take a good look at the lovely ballroom on the third floor.

RINDGE (via US 202 and SR 119): The elevated setting of Rindge provides beautiful views of the surrounding hills and mountains. **Cathedral of the Pines** is a non-sectarian memorial to American servicemen killed in battle. The main Cathedral section is entirely outdoors and has stones donated from each of the 50 states and from many Presidents. There's also a bell tower and two structures holding state and foreign flags and war memorabilia. Attractive landscaped pathways lead to several gardens and other smaller chapels. The extensive grounds and exhibits require about an hour of your time.

The Sunapee Area

Between Claremont and Franklin

NEWPORT (on SR 11): The **Library Arts Center** features changing exhibits on both fine arts and local and regional history.

SUNAPEE (on SR 11): This town is a popular and picturesque resort centered around Lake Sunapee. Naturally, boat rides on the lake are a prime activity and you can cruise it on the *MV Mt. Sunapee* for 1½ hours. There are good views of several islands and the surrounding mountains. At **Mt. Sunapee State Park**, summer visitors can use the ski chairlifts to ascend 2,743-foot Mt. Sunapee, where the observation platform has great views of the entire region. The park also has an extensive system of trails. Allow about 45 minutes for the chairlift, but more if you intend to go hiking.

WARNER (via I-89 and SR 103): The **Mt. Kearsage Indian Museum** is New England's only museum devoted to native American culture. The extensive exhibits, including many dioramas, are seen on a 90-minute guided tour. **The Medicine Woods** cover two acres and display plants, herbs and shrubs used by the natives for food and medicine as well as clothing dyes. **Rollins State Park** has a scenic road that climbs up the southern slope of Mt. Kearsage. From the end of the road there's an easy half-mile trail that leads to the granite summit, which is devoid of vegetation. Allow about an hour for the combined round trip drive and walk.

The White Mountains

As this region covers almost the entire northern half of the state, check state map for location

HEBRON (southern White Mountains, about 10 miles from Plymouth): The **Audubon-Paradise Point Nature Center** consists of five different trails along the shore of Newfoundland Lake. There are also wildlife exhibits. Allow a minimum of an hour.

RUMNEY (northwest of Plymouth via SR 25): This small community is known as the home of the founder of Christian Science. The

Mary Baker Eddy Historic House, where she lived in the early 1860s, can be visited.

SUGAR HILL (west of Franconia via SR 117): Explore the history of the town from the earliest settlers right up to its present status as a resort area at the **Sugar Hill Historical Museum**. Several buildings contain furnishings and implements from various periods as well as exhibits. A collection of horse-drawn vehicles is contained in the carriage barn. About 45 minutes should suffice to see everything.

The Lakes Area

North and west of Lake Winnipesaukee

CENTER SANDWICH (via SR 113): The **Sandwich Historical Society & Elisha Marston House** has a varied collection of items covering more than two centuries. Included are antiques, vehicles and implements. Allow about a half-hour.

MOULTONBOROUGH (via SR 25): This town is well known for the **Castle in the Clouds**, a 100-year-old mansion built in the Ossipee Mountains and overlooking Lake Winnipesaukee, which is several miles away. The severe-looking house is the focal point of a 5,200-acre estate and was designed to provide a spectacular view from any room. The estate also is the source of Castle Springs Water and you can visit the bottling plant. Hiking trails and horseback rides are available. Plan on spending between one and two hours, depending upon your activities outside the house. The house can be seen by self-guiding tour.

WAKEFIELD (via SR 109 from the southeastern end of the lake): This town represents the furthest point from the suggested itinerary, but the **Museum of Childhood of Wakefield** is a most unusual attraction. The complex includes a one-room schoolhouse, more than 3,000 dolls, stuffed animals and doll houses, along with many sleighs and other items. Between 30 and 45 minutes should be sufficient time for most people to see the museum, but doll lovers might require a bit more.

WOLFBORO (via SRs 11 and 28): Located in a southeastern corner of Lake Winnipesaukee, Wolfboro offers short (1½-hour) cruises on the lake via the *MV Judge Sewall*. The trips concentrate on a portion of the lake not fully explored on trips from Weirs Beach. The town itself has a number of interesting museums and historic sites. The **Wright Museum – A Museum of American Enterprise** covers the home front during the years of World War II and shows how American ingenuity helped us get through the crisis of that time. Allow about 30 minutes. At the **Wolfboro Historical Society Museum** you can relive many aspects of 19th-century life in about a half-hour. There is a small school, fire engines, wagons, a farm house and more. The natural history of the area can be explored at the **Libby Museum**. Besides mounted specimens of local wildlife, the museum explores the culture of the Abenaki Indians. The home of the last colonial governor of New Hampshire can be seen at the **Governor John Wentworth Historic Site**. Finally, taking a breather from museums, you might want to see the **Hampshire Pewter Company,** where factory tours take you through a process of pewter making that was used in the 16th century. The quality of the work is unmistakable. Tours last about a half-hour.

Vermont

The Green Mountain State

Everywhere you go in Vermont you will find small towns nestled in the woods and among the lakes of this serene state. While it doesn't have the coastline of Maine and the mountains and geologic formations aren't as high or as unusual as those in neighboring New Hampshire, Vermont has plenty of scenery. Much of it is part of the Green Mountain National Forest.

It is a land where the memory of yesterday is still very much alive. Tradition remains strong in this part of the country. You'll feel you are returning to a simpler time when you visit Vermont and perhaps that is its great attraction.

Along the Suggested Itinerary

Our journey through Vermont will begin in **Burlington** because, as the state's largest city (but with a population barely reaching 40,000), more airlines fly in here than to any other Vermont airport. There's a good chance, however, that you'll be joining our loop at a different point if you come in by car. The western border of Vermont adjoins New York State and can be entered at several points. Those originating from along the eastern seaboard will probably join the route at Vermont's southern border. Another possibility is to fly into Boston and drive to Vermont from there. It's only about 120 miles – not a great deal considering the limited amount of mileage to be covered within Vermont. Therefore, that option is still very viable.

Burlington's airport is only three miles from the center of the city, reached by taking US 2 westbound. That road becomes Main Street and we'll begin our explorations there. Burlington is on the shores of Lake Champlain, the state's largest lake, and it slopes downward toward the lakefront, making it a very attractive city.

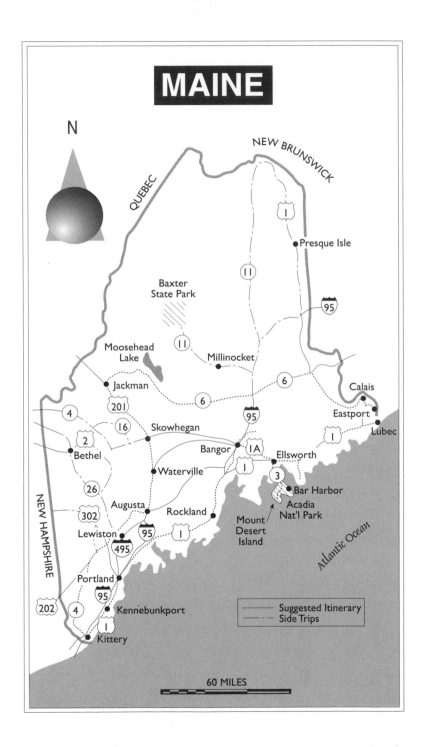

The **Robert H. Fleming Museum**, on the campus of the University of Vermont, has both permanent and changing fine art collections. After exploring the museum and the attractive campus, which together should take about 45 minutes, head down Pearl Street toward the lake. At the very end of the street is **Battery Park**, so called because during the War of 1812, American artillery batteries engaged the British fleet here. The park provides an excellent vantage point for viewing the lake and is the site of concerts during the summer.

A ride on Lake Champlain is a must during any visit to Burlington. One of the most popular lake cruises is on the *Spirit of Ethan Allen*, built in the style of a Mississippi sternwheeler. The narrated voyage will point out the sights and relate them to the events of the Revolutionary War era. The trip takes 90 minutes. While there are other boat tours offering similar journeys, an interesting and cheaper alternative way to see the lake is to take one of the ferries that connect Burlington with New York State on the lake's western shore. These trips vary, depending upon destination, from 12 to 60 minutes one way. Service is frequent.

North of downtown Burlington is the **Ethan Allen Homestead**. It's about two miles from the Battery. From the corner of Pearl and Champlain Streets, head north on Champlain until you reach SR 127, then follow signs that will take you directly to the Homestead. The almost legendary Green Mountain Boys were involved in disputes between New Hampshire and New York over Vermont until the common enemy of the Revolution turned their attention to harassing the British. Ethan Allen was their leader. Besides the small 1787 furnished home, there's a multimedia show on the history of the region, concentrating on Ethan Allen, of course, as well as gardens and trails. Allow a minimum of an hour. Nearby in **Ethan Allen Park** there is an observation tower with lake and mountain views.

Back to Burlington for a moment to consider shopping and other matters. For a city of its size, Burlington has a wealth of shops. The best place to go is the **Church Street Marketplace** in the historic downtown district. The Marketplace consists of a four-block pedestrian mall, with more than 130 stores and 20 restaurants. Within the Marketplace is the Burlington Square Mall, another shopping complex.

> *Plenty of places to spend the night can be found in and around Burlington, including many of the major chains. Prices are low compared to some of Vermont's resort areas. Dining is also plentiful, and you might want to consider one of the many restaurants in a variety of price ranges that you will find within the Church Street Marketplace.*

Leave Burlington via I-89, taking it briefly north to Exit 17. Then hop on US 2 westbound (although most of your trip on it will be north if you look at a compass). US 2 will take you over five bridges across Lake Champlain, connecting several of the picturesque Lake Champlain islands. The route is a scenic one, providing vistas of not only the lake but of New York's Adirondack Mountains to the west and Vermont's Green Mountains to the east.

First and largest of the islands is **Grand Isle**. Right on US 2 is the **Hyde Log Cabin**. Built in 1783, it is believed to be the oldest existing original log cabin still standing in the United States. It is furnished in period to show what rural life in the 18th century would have been like.

Next comes the island of **North Hero**. The attraction here, besides the quaint atmosphere, is the summer home of the **Royal Lipizzan Stallions of Austria**. These are the same famous horses who have dazzled audiences in Vienna's Hofburg Palace complex. The beauty of these animals, as well as the discipline and intelligence necessary to perform the intricate and graceful maneuvers ordered by their riders, will amaze and thrill all ages. Performances are limited during the stallions' early July to Labor Day residence in Vermont. Call (802) 372-5683 for information on performance times and tickets. You should make every effort to see the Lippizzaners. Performances last around an hour.

Continuing north through the lake route, stay on US 2 until the town of South Alburg. Then take SR 129 for five miles to Isle LaMotte, where you'll visit **St. Anne's Shrine**. The beautiful grounds contain a chapel and grotto, a walk depicting the Stations of the Cross and statues of Our Lady of Lourdes and Samuel de Champlain. The latter statue was carved in nearby Montreal for Expo 67. The Shrine is on the site of Fort Anne, the oldest settlement in Vermont. Allow about 45 minutes.

Now return to US 2 and continue west on it until the junction of SR 78. Follow SR 78 for 10 miles to the town of Swanton, only seven miles from the Canadian border. The entrance to the **Missiquoi National Wildlife Refuge** is on SR 78. A 1½-mile nature trail gives you the opportunity to observe a variety of wildlife, especially waterfowl, along the level and easy walk. Allow at least a half-hour.

Immediately east of Swanton is I-89. Take it south to Exit 19. The spur off of the highway at this exit will lead you directly onto Main Street in St. Albans. The **St. Albans Historical Museum** is in a former school building constructed in the mid-1860's. Both Revolutionary and Civil War artifacts constitute an important part of the collection (St. Albans was a station of the Underground Railway during the Civil War). A room of the museum has been furnished to conform exactly to one of Norman Rockwell's paintings. Mr. Rockwell was fond of using Vermont scenes in his works and you'll encounter more of him later on in the trip. Allow 30-45 minutes for the museum.

Head back towards the Interstate, but turn right on SR 104 just before the freeway interchange and continue for 20 miles to Jeffersonville. Paintings of typical New England scenery can be seen in a brief stop at the **Mary Bryan Memorial Art Gallery**. From town head south on SR 108, also known as the 10th Mountain Division Memorial Highway. This will bring you into the heart of some of Vermont's most beautiful country as you approach the Mt. Mansfield-Stowe region. **Smugglers Notch State Park** is a deep, rugged and very winding pass containing many unusual rock formations, as well as attractive Bingham Falls.

> *This area, including the resort complex that also goes by the name of Smugglers Notch, is teeming with accommodations of every type and price range.*

The northern approach to Mt. Mansfield that you're on is usually closed in winter due to heavy snowfall. Mount Mansfield is the crowning jewel of the Green Mountains and Vermont's highest peak. Soaring to almost 4,400 feet, the mountain stretches for five miles. Most of the best scenery is located within **Mount Mansfield State Park**. There are those who claim that the mountain resembles a human face, but it takes a great deal of imagination to see that.

On the other hand, it takes no imagination to see the beauty from the popular Long Trail that goes to the summit. Although you may not want to hike all the way, even the lower portion of the trail is worthwhile. The unpaved **Stowe Auto Road** covers almost five miles and is a fairly difficult toll road because of steep grades and sharp turns. It climbs to near the summit of Mt. Mansfield, where you'll find more trails and the best scenery. Allow a minimum of 90 minutes to explore Mt. Mansfield State Park. (An entire day is needed if you intend to hike the entire length of the Long Trail and return the same way.)

An easier way to see things from the top is via the **Stowe Gondola**. The small gondola cars (four passengers each) will whisk you to the summit, where you'll find crisp mountain air and the unspoiled beauty of nature. Small farms and towns are also visible below. Allow at least a half-hour for the round-trip and some time to take in the gorgeous vistas. Adjacent to the gondola is the **Stowe Alpine Slide,** where a chairlift takes you to the top of the slide. You control the speed of the descent. Children will especially love seeing the mountain in this manner.

About 10 miles south of Mt. Mansfield at the end of SR 108 is the bustling resort town of **Stowe**. Home to outdoor activities, including golf, tennis, fishing, canoeing and just about everything else, Stowe is also the beginning point of the **Stowe Recreation Path**, a five-mile scenic walkway along the edge of a mountain stream. Time allotment depends upon how much of the path you intend to walk, but allow a half-hour per mile. The walk is easy.

From Stowe, head north on SR 100 for 10 miles to Morrisville. At the junction of SR 15 is the **LaMoille Valley Railroad**. Both one- and two-hour excursions are offered that take you through a variety of scenery along the LaMoille River. You'll see mountains and rivers as well as numerous farms and villages as you ride in open-air coaches. The short trip passes a beautiful waterfall while the longer ride will take you over a covered bridge – the only one still carrying a railroad in the United States. Within town is the **Morrisville Noyes House Historical Museum**, which depicts 19th-century life through artifacts and furnishings in this stately mansion. Allow about a half-hour.

Now proceed east on SR 15 for 10 miles to Wolcott. Here you can see the railroad's covered bridge if you missed it in taking the one-hour trip. A few miles past Wolcott go north on SR 14 for 12 miles to Craftsbury. If you ask a hundred people which is their favorite Vermont or New England village you're liable to get a hundred different answers. But just about everyone could agree that the **Craftsbury Common**, with its village green surrounded by attractive buildings, is *the* typical New England village. Take a few moments to stroll about town and perhaps get a bite to eat.

Continue north on SR 14 to the junction of US 5, then go north on the latter for 11 miles to Newport. You'll find dining and accommodations here. The town is at the very southern tip of Lake Memphremagog (meaning "beautiful waters" in the local Indian dialect), the greater portion of which lies in the Canadian province of Quebec. The view of the lake is lovely. In town, take Indian Street to Bluff Road and the **American Maple Products Company**. You'll be guided through the factory, which makes maple candy, and be given delicous samples. Tours take 30 minutes.

Ten miles further north on US 5 is Derby Line, right on the Canadian border. In fact, the **Haskell Free Library and Opera House** is unique in that the stage is in Canada while the audience sits in the United States! Inquire at the box office if you're interested in seeing an opera.

From Derby Line head south on I-91 to Exit 26, then proceed east on SR 58 to the town of Orleans. Follow signs for the town of Brownington, 2½ miles north of Orleans. The **Old Stone House Museum** is a large four-story structure built in the mid-1830's. It was originally a school dormitory and now houses a local history museum. But its 23 rooms of exhibits make it bigger than many of this genre, so take at least 45 minutes to browse around.

Return to I-95, heading south for one exit to Barton. The **Sugarmill Farm and Museum** is just what the name implies. You'll tour the farm with its maple orchards, then go into the mill and see how maple syrup is manufactured and packaged, before proceeding to the museum, which chronicles the history of maple syrup making. The grounds also include attractive fish ponds and you can even go for a ride on a hay wagon, which children will certainly enjoy. Allow at least an hour. Our route will take us to many such maple manufacturing enterprises and you would go crazy if you tried to see them all. However, Vermont is definitely the maple syrup capital of the country and you should check out at least one or two. This particular one, because of the diversity of things to see and do, a prime candidate.

Leave Barton via SR 16, heading south for three miles to Glover, then drive a half-mile on SR 122 to the **Bread and Puppet Museum**. Located in a large barn, various puppet shows are performed to delight the children and even many adults. If you're lucky, you'll arrive during one of the larger pageants, where the town's residents get into the act.

Go back on SR 16 north to I-91. Take I-91 south for 28 miles to Exit 21 and the town of **St. Johnsbury**.

> *One of the larger communities in this part of the state, the industrial town of St. Johnsbury has a scenic setting and, with its variety of lodging and dining options, is a good place to stop overnight.*

The first attraction in town of note is the **Fairbanks Museum and Planetarium** (Main and Prospect Streets), the only public planetarium in the state. The Victorian-style building houses, in addition to the planetarium show, the Northern New England Weather Center, a Children's Nature Corner and over 4,500 mounted animal specimens. Give yourself about an hour. Also on Main Street is the **St. Johnsbury Athenaeum Art Gallery**, which focuses on 19th-century artwork.

East of downtown on US 2 is the **Original Maple Grove Museum and Factory**. This one, like the Sugarmill Farm previously mentioned, is also a good choice. It's the world's oldest and largest maple candy factory (or so the owners claim). You'll visit a museum and tour the candy factory, which should take about 30 minutes.

Leave St. Johnsbury via US 2, heading west for 19 miles to SR 215 and then north for five miles to the town of Cabot. The **Cabot Creamery** offers a video about plant operations and then you can look through observation windows and see the manufacture of butter and cheese. After all, one cannot live by maple syrup and candy alone!

Now head back to US 2 westbound for about 10 miles to the junction of SR 14, where you'll soon reach **Barre**, one of Vermont's larger "cities," with almost 10,000 residents.

> *Barre has many places to stay and a number of good restaurants too.*

Known throughout the world for the fine granite products made here, the famous **Rock of Ages** can be reached by staying on SR 14 for three miles south of Barre and then via signs to the quarry in Graniteville. The world's largest granite quarry (a hole nearly 500 feet deep and covering almost 60 acres) has an interesting visitor center that explains the quarrying process. Follow this with a visit to the observation deck, where you watch the granite being cut and polished. The tours are self-guided and you can walk or take a short train ride to the quarry site. Allow almost an hour to see everything at the Rock of Ages – an interesting experience for all ages.

The nearby state capital of **Montpelier** can be reached easily from the Rock of Ages by going back on SR 14 to the junction of US 302 and then heading west on the latter for five miles. Where US 302 meets US 2, turn left and proceed until you reach the Main Street Bridge. Cross the bridge and you're in the heart of town. This is the nation's smallest capital city. Besides government, it's also a major commercial center for the state.

> *You can find a good selection of accommodations in Montpelier.*

The **State Capitol** on State Street is built, of course, with granite from Barre. The impressive Doric-style building is crowned with a gold dome and a statue of Ceres, goddess of agriculture (Vermont's rural way of life is evident in so many ways). Guided tours of the building are given or you can wander about on your own. Either way, allow about a half-hour. The capitol area contains a number of architecturally interesting and attractive public buildings. Close by, also on State Street, is the **Vermont Historical Society**, where varied and changing exhibits will take you through the state's long and colorful history, with an emphasis on its people and towns.

If you haven't had enough maple syrup yet, two more factories are in the Montpelier area. These are the **Morse Farm and Sugarhouse** (three miles north of the State House) and **Danforth's Sugarhouse** (on US 2 east of the city). However, we're going to be heading to our next destination by going back across the bridge and turning right on Memorial Drive, which runs into I-89. Take the Interstate north to Exit 10 and the town of **Waterbury**. At the exit go north on SR 100 for a mile. You've had plenty of candy and syrup, and even some butter and cheese. But wait for the gastronomic delights you'll find in Waterbury! First there is **Ben and Jerry's Ice Cream Factory**. Thirty-minute tours explain the entire process of how this popular ice cream is made. You can buy ice cream here as well. Also on SR 100 is the **Cold Hollow Cider Mill**, where you can see how apple cider is made and sample some of the products.

Now it's time to leave Waterbury by heading south on SR 100, officially known as the 43rd Infantry Division Memorial Highway. This is Vermont's longest road, winding its way from the Canadian border to the Massachusetts state line. It is also one of the state's most scenic routes as it traverses the Green Mountains and the Green Mountain National Forest.

About 17 miles south of Waterbury is the small town of **Warren**. Situated on the eastern edge of the Green Mountain National Forest a few miles south of town is the **Granville Gulf State Park**. There's a six-mile scenic drive through the gulf (another local term for "notch") that will enable you to see the Mad River making its way to pretty Moss Glen Falls. The falls has one large drop, followed by several smaller ones. Allow about a half-hour. A few miles south of the State Park turn right on SR 125, which will take you into the **Green Mountain National Forest**. It covers more than 350,000 acres in two major sections of central and southern Vermont and includes six separate wilderness areas. There are more than 500 miles of trails.

The first stop on SR 125 is the **Texas Falls Recreation Area**. There is an observation platform from which to view the falls, along with a nice nature trail. The **Robert Frost Wayside** and the **Robert Frost Trail** come soon after. (The highway in this area is called the Robert Frost Memorial Drive.) There are good views of the mountains from the wayside and the trail is an easy one, where you can see flora typical of the region. The road itself is also an attraction, especially when it passes through Middlebury Gap. This round-trip detour onto SR 125 can be completed in about 90 minutes. Although you can skip it entirely by simply remaining on SR 100, it's well worth the time and it offers some of the best Green Mountain scenery on the route.

After returning to SR 100, follow the scenic route south once again through mountains and picturesque towns for 25 miles to the town of Sherburne, more commonly known as **Killington**. This is one of Vermont's most popular year-round resorts, especially renowned for its excellent winter skiing. On the way in, you'll go over Sherburne Pass, nearly 2,200 feet above sea level.

> *The town and resort area has numerous accommodations, many in the form of mountain lodges. Rates tend to be on the pricey side.*

There's golf, tennis, hiking, boating, and fishing. The **Killington Ski & Summer Resort**, west of town on US 4, contains both a gondola and a chairlift, the base stations being about four miles apart. Only the chairlift operates in summer. The 1¼-mile ride takes about a half-hour up and back. Nearby is the **Pico Alpine Slide**. You reach the top of the slide via another chairlift.

Continue southbound on SR 100 to **Plymouth** and take SR 100A to the **Plymouth Notch Historic District/Birthplace of Calvin Coolidge**. The site contains both the house in which the President was born and the one he grew up in. There are original furnishings in both. The visitor center has exhibits on Coolidge and local history. A number of other buildings typical of an early 20th-century Vermont village are also here. Allow about 1¼ hours to see it all.

Take SR 100A north to the junction of US 4 and then head east on US 4 for eight miles to the pretty town of **Woodstock**.

> *Varied accommodations can be found in Woodstock, as well as in the next several towns along the itinerary.*

On your way into and out of Woodstock you'll encounter several covered bridges. There are two attractions just north of town via SR 12. One is the **Dana House**, the local historical society, with exhibits on more than 250 years of regional life and events. Allow about 30 minutes. The **Billings Farm and Museum** is a working dairy farm. Of equal interest is the museum, housed in four large barns. Each barn represents a season of the year and together they take you through the complete annual agricultural cycle. Another building was once the farm manager's house and it has been restored to its 1890 appearance. Because of the diversity of attractions here, give yourself at least 90 minutes.

Another highly recommended place to visit in Woodstock is the **Vermont Raptor Center**, located at the Vermont Institute of Natural Science on Church Hill Road. The center is home to eagles, falcons, hawks and owls that cannot be released into the wild because of various injuries that they've sustained. The visitor center explains how the birds are cared for and you can observe them on nature trails that wind through the 72-acre center. Allow 45-60 minutes for this fascinating place. Also in town is **Sugarbush Farms**, another maple syrup and cheese factory, if you haven't already had enough of that sort of thing.

Several miles east of Woodstock, still on US 4, is **Quechee Gorge**. Known affectionately as "Vermont's Little Grand Canyon," the gorge is 162 feet deep and is best viewed from walkways on the US 4 bridge that spans the mile-long chasm. There's also a trail along the rim of the gorge which will bring you past a waterfall. You should be able to cover the gorge in 30-45 minutes. Still on US 4 near the gorge is **Timber Village**, a most unusual shopping area. The Village has hundreds of shops featuring antiques and collectibles of every conceivable type. Hundreds more artisans display their works here as well. For children, or once you're through shopping, a miniature railroad, horse-drawn hay rides or sleigh rides are among the diversions here. You should figure on spending at least 90 minutes at Timber Village, especially if you're traveling with children or if you're a compulsive shopper.

A couple of miles further east on US 4 is the town of **White River Junction**, at the confluence of the White and Connecticut Rivers, across from New Hampshire. The **Catamount Brewing Company** (on South Main off US 4) is a new facility that produces old-style English ales. The factory tour takes you through the brewing process and the history of brewing in New England. Samples are available at the end of the tour, which requires approximately 45 minutes.

Take I-91 on the west edge of town south to Exit 9 (about 10 miles) and then use US 5 south for the short ride along the Connecticut River into **Windsor**. The **Old Constitution House** is an 18th-century tavern, important in Vermont's history because it was the site where Vermont's 1777 Constitution was signed. Exhibits describing the event and other important aspects of Vermont's history are featured. It's one of the state's more interesting historical museums and you should allow about 45 minutes. A mile south of town on US 5 is the **Simon Pearce Glass Works**. From a viewing gallery above the 33,000-square-foot facility, you can see the entire process by which fine glass is hand-blown. There's a retail shop where you can buy their glass products. Allow 30 minutes.

Four miles south of the glass works is the junction with SR 131. Head west for 17 miles to **Proctorsville**. Then go north on SR 103 and in half a mile you'll reach the **Joseph Cerniglia Winery**. Guided tours (30 minutes) take you through the wine-making process and free tastings are given at the end. Then continue north on SR 103 to **Ludlow**. On High Street is the interesting **Black River Academy Museum**. The Academy had a fine reputation for over a hundred years. Now, the museum traces the school's history and that of some of its more famous graduates as well as showing what life was like in rural Vermont during the 19th century.

From Ludlow you'll get back on SR 100, heading south once more on the still scenic route. It's only 10 miles to your next destination in Weston. Two attractions right on SR 100 are worth brief stops. The **Vermont Country Store**, an 1890's general store, features goods of that time period. The **Guild of Old Time Crafts and Industries** is in a sawmill dating from the late 18th century. Artisans are at work using old-time tools.

A short distance south of Weston is the village of Londonderry, where you'll head east on SR 11 for 20 miles to **Springfield**.

> *Both accommodations and dining facilities can be found here in Springfield.*

To the east of town, towards I-91, is the interesting **Stellafane Society Museum**. James Hartness, an inventor and astronomer, lived here after the turn of the century. The most fascinating part of your visit is the trip from the main house via a tunnel almost 250 feet long to a five-room underground apartment containing telescopes and other items relating to astronomy. Several telescopes on the grounds are still in working order and can be used. Allow 30 minutes.

SR 11 will bring you to the intersection of I-91, where you'll head south to Exit 6 (about six miles) and the village of **Rockingham**, just west of the highway. There's a branch of the Vermont Country Store located here, but the main reason for leaving the Interstate is to visit the **Old Rockingham Meeting House**, a church dating from 1787. Both the pulpit and pews are of an unusual design and the cemetery surrounding the structure has many headstones that recreate the town's history.

Head back towards the Interstate, but don't get on it. Instead, drive south on US 5, which parallels the highway and will soon bring you into **Bellows Falls**. The falls that gave the town its name aren't much to see these days, but a two-hour ride on the **Green Mountain Flyer** is lots of fun. The 26-mile round-trip excursion in restored coaches pulled by a 1930s diesel locomotive goes past the Brockways Mills Gorge and passes many farms, rivers and small towns. You'll see a number of covered bridges too.

> *Bellows Falls has a number of good places to stay.*

From Bellows Falls, take I-91 south to Exit 4 or just stay on US 5 south to the town of **Putney** (the Interstate won't save you any time because the first stop on the itinerary is only a couple of miles north of the interchange). **Santa's Land** is a Christmas-theme village where both children and adults can visit with Santa Claus, Rudolph the reindeer and other characters. A petting zoo and numerous rides and shows are also available. You might not want to stop here if you're traveling without children; otherwise, it will be hard to drag the tots away before at least an hour and perhaps double that. In town is **Basketville**, a factory where baskets have been made by hand for more than 150 years. There's also a factory store.

> *Accommodations and dining are available in Putney.*

Now drive south on I-91 for 10 miles to Exit 2 and then east into **Brattleboro**, one of the state's largest towns, with more than 12,000 people. Brattleboro is also the closest point in Vermont to Boston, so if you rented a car at Logan International Airport, you'll join the suggested itinerary here. Follow SR 9 east (Western Avenue) to Main Street and the **Brattleboro Museum and Art Center**. Galleries house changing art exhibits, but a permanent feature is on the works of Rudyard Kipling, who lived in Brattleboro for several years. The attractively restored building once served as the Union Railroad Station. Give yourself about a half-hour.

Take SR 9 in a westerly direction. This very scenic route travaerses the southern portion of the state. Beginning about 10 miles from Brattleboro, the section between Marlboro and Wilmington is especially attractive, and the views from Hogback Mountain are outstanding. Upon reaching Wilmington, turn right and go north on SR 100 (your final time on this road) for 10 miles to Mt. Snow. In an especially scenic portion of the Green Mountains, this is one of Vermont's most famous recreation areas. The **Mt. Snow Ski Area** offers a chairlift that operates in summer for the 1½-mile trip to the 3,600-foot summit. You can see parts of four different states from this vantage point. The round-trip to the top and some time for taking in the scenery requires about 45 minutes.

> *Summer accommodations in and around Mt. Snow are available at fairly reasonable rates.*

Return to SR 9 and continue west once again. The route remains scenic (going through a wide belt of the Green Mountain National Forest). Upon leaving the forest you'll arrive in **Bennington**, the state's third largest city and one of the most historic. The Battle of Bennington was a critical victory for the Americans in the Revolutionary War.

On US 9 is West Main Street and shortly after arriving in town you'll come to the **Bennington Museum**. The building contains an unusual collection of Americana but is most noted for the large number of works by Grandma Moses. Allow about 45 minutes. Proceed further down Main Street and turn right onto Monument Avenue. At the end of the street is the **Bennington Battle Monument**. Built in 1891, the granite shaft is 306 feet high, making it the tallest structure in Vermont. An elevator takes visitors to the top where, despite rather small windows, you get a very good view of the town, surrounding valley and mountains. The Monument also contains a diorama and exhibits that describe the Battle of Bennington. You should spend no longer than a half-hour at the Monument. Also located on Monument Avenue is the **Old First Church**, constructed in the early 1800s and considered by many to be one of the most attractive churches in New England. Many famous Vermont residents, including Robert Frost, are buried here.

> There are few chain motels in Bennington but you will find many small independent guesthouses and B&Bs, along with a variety of good restaurants.

In North Bennington, reached via US 7 (in downtown Bennington) and then by SRs 7A and 67A, is the **Park-McCullough House**. The name represents two prominent Vermont families, who provided two of the state's governors. The 1865 mansion contains 35 rooms filled with original furnishings, antiques and works of art. The house is considered an excellent example of the French Second Empire style. Surrounding the house are attractive gardens. There is also a carriage and sleigh barn. Listed on the National Register of Historic Places, the house should take between 45 minutes and an hour to visit.

Now continue on SR 67A to SR 7A northbound, known as the Ethan Allen Highway, for 12 miles to Arlington. Here is the **Norman Rockwell Exhibit**, housing hundreds of covers created by Rockwell for *The Saturday Evening Post*. Other works of the long-time Vermont resident are also part of the exhibit, which is in a 19th-century church.

SR 7A becomes very scenic after Arlington, with fine views of the National Forest to the east on the drive towards **Manchester**. You'll soon be in the shadow of Mt. Equinox on your left. There are several worthwhile attractions near Manchester. First, there is **Mt. Equinox** itself. Part of the Taconic Range, the mountain is 3,816 feet high. There are wonderful views from the summit, which can be reached by a five-mile paved road. There are some steep grades and serious turns, but only the novice driver is likely to have a problem with them. Just take it slow. Allow 45-60 minutes to make the round-trip, including some time at the top to take in the view.

Three miles north of the cutoff road for Mt. Equinox (back on SR 7A) is **Hildene**, which served as a summer home for a son of Abraham Lincoln and his descendents until about 20 years ago. The beautiful Georgian-style mansion has been kept in perfect condition and contains many original Lincoln family furnishings and memorabilia. There are 24 rooms in the house, along with spacious lawns and formal gardens that provide good vantage points to enjoy the beautiful surrounding scenery. One of Hildene's most interesting features is a 1,000-pipe organ. The Carriage House has been converted into a visitor center, where you'll find interesting exhibits and a slide presentation. Allow about 90 minutes for the guided house tour and for browsing about on your own outside.

Within Manchester town is the **Southern Vermont Art Center,** located in a sprawling former mansion on an estate covering about 400 acres. The Center houses a variety of artworks, but of greater interest to many visitors is the outdoor sculpture garden and botany trail. Allow a minimum of 30 minutes. The last of the town's attractions will be a must for the fisherman in your party – the **American Museum of Fly Fishing** on SR 7A. Covering all aspects of the sport, the museum's most unusual items are the tackle used by various U.S. Presidents and celebrities.

A few miles north of Manchester, SR 7A runs into US 7. Continue on that road north a total of about 20 miles from Manchester to Wallingford, where you should turn right (east) onto SR 140. Three miles east of town on the state route is **White Rocks.** This recreation area, inside the National Forest, includes a trail to the unusual rocks and there are excellent views of nearby mountain summits and valleys. Allow about 45 minutes before returning to US 7 and continuing north for 11 more miles into **Rutland.**

> *Rutland is a popular destination for visitors to Vermont and has a variety of lodgings at various price ranges, along with many good places to eat.*

Known as the "Marble City" because of nearby quarries (which we'll get to shortly), the town houses the **Norman Rockwell Museum of Vermont** on US 4 (Woodstock Avenue) about two miles east of the junction with US 7 (Main Street). The museum is the largest one devoted to the numerous and varied works of the artist, who spent many years in Vermont. More than 2,000 works are shown, covering his more than 60-year career. Included are magazine covers, advertisements, and book illustrations. You don't have to be an art lover to enjoy Rockwell's works – no doubt that's what made his works so popular. So give yourself about an hour to explore the museum.

Off US 4 on the west side of town, then north in **Proctor** via West Proctor Road, is the unusual **Wilson Castle**. The 32-room brick castle, complete with turret, parapet and many open arches, was built in the late 1860s on a 115-acre estate. The house is a virtual art museum with valuable items from all over the world. Also of note are the many stained glass windows and tile fireplaces. There are also extensive grounds that can be explored on your own, but the castle itself is only visited by a guided tour. Allow 75-90 minutes.

Within the town of Proctor itself, on Main Street, is the **Vermont Marble Exhibit**. The extensive displays cover the entire history of Vermont's important marble industry. Beautiful marble works are also on display and you can watch craftsmen at work. Various films on the industry are shown continuously. Allow about an hour to visit the exhibit. SR 3 leads north out of Proctor and back into US 7. A bit further north is the town of **Pittsford**, where the **New England Maple Museum** is located. It's been a while since we've encountered one of these, so it may be time for another quick "fix." There's also a **Federal Fish Hatchery** nearby that stocks Lake Champlain and the Connecticut River with Atlantic Salmon.

Approximately seven miles north of Pittsford, leave US 7 (at Brandon) via SR 73 heading east. A couple of miles later at Forest Dale, turn left onto SR 53 for the short ride to two scenic attractions within the National Forest. The first is the **Falls of Lana**, where the Silver Lake Trail (one mile round-trip) will take you past the Falls and through a very picturesque area. Then go back to Forest Dale and continue east on SR 73 for a little while to **Brandon Gap**. Here you'll get an excellent vista from the Mt. Horrid Observation Site. The view is anything but horrid! Near Brandon Gap is the town of **Goshen**, where many people like to pick wild berries from the fields (it's allowed as long as you're not on private property).

Now you can work your way back to US 7; from Brandon it's 17 miles to your next destination, another of Vermont's popular tourist areas – the town of **Middlebury**. Summer programs at Middlebury College, established in 1800, are renowned throughout the country. The **Sheldon Museum**, a 19th-century structure, has rooms furnished with period decor and traces life in Vermont over the course of two centuries. Allow about 45 minutes. Then take SR 23 north from town and follow signs for a total distance of three miles to the **UVM Morgan Horse Farm**. The Morgan Horse was the first breed of horse to be developed in America and has since become Vermont's state animal. Set on rolling pastureland and woods, the complex houses over 60 of the Morgan breed in barns of an attractive architectural style. You are told about the history of the breed and there is a tour through the working horse farm. Plan on spending about an hour.

Return to Middlebury and pick up US 7 north again for 12 miles to **Vergennes**. This small town has a number of historic buildings and you might want to take a quick stroll through the historic district. Also consider a visit to the **Factory Marketplace at Kennedy Brothers**, a former creamery that now has more than 150 different craft booths. It's one of many unusual places to shop throughout Vermont. Then follow marked signs from the junction of US 7 and SR 22A to the tiny community of **Basin Harbor**, on the shore of Lake Champlain. The **Lake Champlain Maritime Museum** has many exhibits describing the history of the Lake and the Champlain Valley area. A 19th-century school building is where most of the exhibits are found, but there's also a boathouse with many types of watercraft manufactured locally over the past 150 years. A highlight of your visit, which should take at least an hour, is a full-size replica of the *Philadelphia*, Benedict Arnold's gunboat, which sank in Lake Champlain in 1776. The replica can be boarded.

Upon returning to Vergennes, head north once again on US 7 for four miles to Ferrisburg. The **Rokeby Museum** was the former residence of author and naturalist, Rowland Robinson. The late 19th-century house is furnished with family belongings and the grounds of the museum also have five old farm buildings. Allow about 45 minutes. And now, what you've all been waiting for – your chance to visit a cheese and maple syrup factory one more time. **Dakin Farm** also manufactures several other types of foods. You can see them all being made, get samples and view exhibits on the production process.

Several miles further north via US 7 is **Charlotte**. Here is the attractive six-acre **Vermont Wildflower Farm**. A self-guiding trail leads through the colorful plantings, which highlight seasonal changes in the flora. There's also a multimedia show, so give yourself at least 45 minutes to tour the farm.

Just north of Charlotte is **Shelburne**. Because of the variety of things to see and do here, you may want to take advantage of the overnight accommodations available in town. Or you could continue on to Burlington, less than 15 minutes away.

The **Vermont Teddy Bear Company**, whose plush jointed bears are seen throughout the nation, is on US 7 immediately south of town. There is an interesting tour that takes you through the entire process of producing these lovable toys. You can, of course, buy a teddy bear to take home or have one shipped anywhere you want. The tours take 45 minutes.

Also on US 7 is the **Shelburne Museum**, the premier Vermont life museum in the state and one of the outstanding museums of its type in the United States. It has a noted collection of American arts, crafts, and architecture. Set on 45 sprawling acres, the 37 different buildings display more than 80,000 objects. Many of the buildings were originally from other parts of New England, disassembled, moved, and meticulously reassembled on this site. Among the more unusual items are a private railroad car and locomotive, and a model circus parade, containing thousands of pieces and measuring over 500 feet in length. There are also extensive grounds and gardens traversed by footpaths (one crosses a covered wooden bridge) and you can even see a sidewheeler, the *S.S. Ticonderoga*, which had to be dragged over land to get it to the Museum. An absolute minimum time for visiting the Shelburne Museum is 2½ hours. But to see everything in detail could well mean spending close to an entire day. However long you stay, it will be time well spent. You could acquire a good understanding of Vermont life by exploring this museum alone.

Shelburne Farms is 1½ miles west of town on a 1,000-acre estate. The working farm is designed to teach agricultural management, but you can observe small farm animals or take a hay ride in addition to the farm tour. The grounds are nicely laid out, having been designed by Frederick Olmstead, who landscaped New York's Central Park. Allow at least an hour.

After Shelburne you'll head back to Burlington via US 7, which leads straight downtown.

Other Attractions

Each of these attractions is close to the main route. In fact, the furthest one-way distance to any place in this section is only about 20 miles. To make things easier, they're broken down by area.

Near the Canadian Border

JAY (16 miles west of Newport via SRs 100 and 101): The **Jay Peak Resort** is a year-round sports and recreation center. In summer you can reach the 4,000-foot summit of Jay Peak by taking the 60-passenger aerial tramway, largest in the state. Excellent vistas of three states and Canada are your reward for the ride. Allow between 45 minutes and an hour.

Burlington-Montpelier Corridor

RICHMOND (12 miles east of Burlington via I-89 to Exit 11 and then by SR 117): The **Old Round Church** only *seems* to be circular. In reality it's a 16-sided polygon. Built in 1813 and recently refurbished to hold special events, the structure was allegedly built by 16 men (each taking a side), with another worker doing the belfry. The story is dubious, at best.

HUNTINGTON and **HUNTINGTON CENTER** (six miles south of Richmond): The **Birds of Vermont Museum** combines models and the real thing to inform visitors about hundreds of species of birds. The museum building has wood-carved birds, each exhibit containing both a male and female as well as the bird's nest and typical habitat. An outdoor bird observation area is on the grounds. Allow a half-hour.

NORTHFIELD (10 miles south of Montpelier via SR 12): **Norwich University Museum** (inside White Memorial Chapel) has many exhibits about this interesting institution, first established as a military college and prominent in the nationwide development of ROTC. The museum highlights the careers of its most famous graduates, including several generals and admirals.

White River Junction Area

SHARON (12 miles northwest of White River Junction via I-89 to Exit 2): The **Joseph Smith Birthplace Memorial** (two miles from Sharon towards Royalton) is a tribute to the founder of the Mormon religion. The large solid piece of granite comprising the monument is set on beautifully landscaped grounds. There's also a visitor center with exhibits and artwork devoted to Smith and Mormonism.

STRAFFORD (eight miles northeast of Sharon via SR 132): The **Justin Smith Morrill Homestead** is the mid-19th-century home of the Vermont Senator who was instrumental in developing the nationwide system of land-grant colleges. The Gothic Revival house has exhibits on Smith and on the land-grant program. Allow about 45 minutes.

NORWICH (five miles north of White River Junction via Exit 13 off I-91): The **Montshire Museum of Science** has exhibits on both the natural and physical sciences. Emphasis is on participatory exhibits. Located on a 100-acre tract by the Connecticut River, the museum also has nature trails and woodlands to be explored. Allow 45 minutes to an hour.

Rutland Vicinity

CASTLETON (eight miles west of Rutland via Exit 4 of US 4): Despite its proximity to both New Hampshire and Massachusetts, scenes of much fighting during the Revolution, relatively little action took place in Vermont. One engagement that did, though, is commemorated at the **Hubbardton Battlefield and Museum**. Various displays explain the course of the battle.

ORWELL (15 miles west of Brandon via SR 73): Another six miles west of town is **Mount Independence**, the site of some Revolutionary War fortifications. The remains of several building foundations are all that are left, but a better reason to come here is to walk the easy trails through nearly 400 acres of varied terrain, with excellent views of Lake Champlain. Allow at least 30 minutes, but more if you intend to do a lot of walking.

Southern Vermont

STRATTON MOUNTAIN (20 miles southeast of Manchester via SR 30 and then following signs): The resort area has all the usual outdoor recreational opportunities that can be found throughout Vermont, but if you're here during the fall, plan on taking in the **Stratton Arts Festival** (typically mid-September to the middle of October), which is one of the largest crafts exhibits of its type.

TOWNSHEND (17 miles northwest of Brattleboro via SR 30): Probably not worth the detour if you've seen a lot of covered bridges. On the other hand, if you're a covered bridge freak, then you'll want to see the unusual three-span bridge on the West River – almost 300 feet in length.

WESTMINSTER (five miles south of Bellows Falls via US 5): The **Westminster MG Car Museum** is said to be the largest privately owned exhibit of a single make of automobile in the world. More than 30 MGs are on display. Allow a minimum of a half-hour.

Addendum 1

Itinerary Outlines

This section summarizes the places visited in each of the three suggested state routes by listing the towns in trip order. For Maine, where side routes are available, these options are graphically depicted. This should enable you to get a quick picture of the possibilities and to customize your trip in a logical fashion. Use these charts in conjunction with the state maps in each chapter or, better still, with a detailed road map. For Maine, the itinerary runs down the left hand side of the page, with side routes being shown at the right, while for New Hampshire and Vermont you can just follow the line.

MAINE

PORTLAND
Scarborough
Orchard Beach
The Biddefords
The Kennebunks
Wells
Ogunquit
The Yorks
Kittery
South Berwick
Springvale
Gray
Gorham ◄────► *Side Trip 1* ◄──────────────► Standish
Poland Springs ◄──► *Side Trip 2* ◄─────► Paris   Sebago Lake
Auburn   Livermore   Naples
Lewiston   Rumford   Fryeburg
Monmouth   Newry   (Return Gorham)
Augusta   Bethel
Waterville   West Paris
                                  (Return Poland Springs)
Skowhegan ◄────► *Side Trip 3* ◄──────────► Farmington
Bingham/Moscow   Rangely
The Forks   Kingfield
Jackman   North Anson
Greenville   (Return Skowhegan)

Howland ←——→ *Side Trip 4* ←————————————→ *Side Trip 5*
Calais　　　　　Baxter State Park　　　　　　　　Houlton
Easport　　　　(Return Howland)　　　　　　　　Presque Isle
Lubec　　　　　　　　　　　　　　　　　　　　　Caribou
Machiasport　　　　　　　　　　　　　　　　　　Van Buren
Columbia Falls　　　　　　　　　　　　　　　　　Madawaska
Schoodic Point　　　　　　　　　　　　　　　　　Fort Kent
Acadia National Park　　　　　　　　　　　　　　Patten
Bar Harbor　　　　　　　　　　　　　　　　　　(Return Howland)
Southwest Harbor
Seal Cove
Ellsworth
Bangor
Orono
Old Town
Prospect
Searsport
Belfast
Camden
Rockport
Rockland
Thomaston
Waldoboro
Damariscotta
Newcastle
Wiscasset
Bath
Brunswick
Freeport
Yarmouth
Falmouth
PORTLAND

NEW HAMPSHIRE

The New Hampshire itinerary that follows includes no side trips.

MANCHESTER, Exeter, Portsmouth, New Castle, Rye, The Hamptons, Seabrook, North Salem, Salem, Nashua, Merrimack, Wilton, Peterborough, Keene, Charlestown, Claremont, Cornish, Hanover, Lebanon, Enfield, Canaan, Grafton, Kinsman Notch, N. Woodstock/Lincoln, North Conway, Glen, Jackson, Bartlett, Crawford Notch, Jefferson, Pinkham Notch, Berlin, Dixville Notch/Colebrook,Littleton, Franconia/Franconia Notch, Plymouth, Holderness, Weirs Beach, Franklin, Canterbury Center, Concord, MANCHESTER

VERMONT

The Vermont itinerary that follows includes no side trips.

BURLINGTON, North Hero, LaMotte, Swanton, St. Albans, Jeffersonville, Mount Mansfield, Stowe, Morrisville, Craftsbury, Newport, Derby Line, Browington,

Barton, Glover, St. Johnsbury, Cabot, Barre, Montpelier, Waterbury, Warren, Killington/Sherburne, Plymouth, Woodstock, Quechee, White River Junction, Windsor, Proctorsville, Ludlow, Weston, Springfield, Rockingham, Bellows Falls, Putney, Brattleboro, Mount Snow, Bennington, North Bennington, Arlington, Manchester Center, Rutland, Proctor, Pittsford, Middlebury, Vergennes, Basin Harbor, Ferrisburg, Charlotte, Shelburne, BURLINGTON

Combining State Itineraries

Earlier it was pointed out that seeing these three states was made much easier by their small size, which keeps the mileage down to reasonable levels for most people. Similarly, the geographic arrangement of Maine, New Hampshire and Vermont makes combining two or even all three states together a snap. While it would take a lengthy trip to cover all three itineraries as suggested in the previous chapters, picking highlights from each of them and making them into a single trip only requires a little careful study of a northern New England Map.

Combining Maine and New Hampshire

Several places along the suggested New Hampshire tour are within close proximity of the Maine state line. The most logical connecting points are:

(1)From **Portsmouth**, NH just skip across the Piscatagua River via I-95 northbound and you're in **Kittery**, Maine, a town which is already on the suggested tour route for that state. Total connection distance is three miles.

(2)From **North Conway**, NH head east on US 302. It's about six miles to the Maine border and the town of **Fryeburg**. Fryeburg is the ending point for one of the Maine side trips, so you're already in sightseeing territory as soon as you cross the border. You can follow the side-trip itinerary or head straight for the main route, which is 40 miles further east, all the way via US 302.

(3)From **Gorham**, NH it's only 22 miles to **Bethel** in Maine and a stop on another side trip from that state. Again, you can ignore the side-route itinerary and head for the main route, the shortest method being SR 26 for 39 miles to Poland Spring.

While the three above connections are the most logical (because they're the shortest and easiest), other routes that could be used are, from south to north: NH SR 25 (from the Lake Winnipesaukee area), which becomes ME SR 25 and leads to the suggested itinerary at Gorham; and NH SR 16 from the western end of Dixville Notch across the Maine line (still SR 16) to Rangely, where it picks up another side trip before joining the suggested itinerary at Skowhegan.

Combining New Hampshire and Vermont

As the Connecticut River forms the New Hampshire/Vermont boundary from the most northerly point in Vermont all the way to where these two states meet the Massachusetts line, it hardly needs an explanation that the itineraries can be joined at any of the 26 bridges that cross the river. However, since several portions of the suggested routes are by the Connecticut River in both states, the most logical connection points, working from south to north, are listed below. The first town shown is on the New Hampshire side of the river, while the second is in Vermont.

(1) Walpole – Bellows Falls
(2) Charlestown – Springfield
(3) Claremont – Ascutney
(4) Cornish – Windsor
(5) Lebanon – White River Junction
(6) Littleton – Lower Waterford (St. Johnsbury area)

All of the towns on the Vermont side are served within a few miles by I-91. On the New Hampshire side, SRs 12 or 12A run along the river, except at Littleton, where I-93 provides direct access.

Directions From Boston

(Logan International Airport)

Since many readers are likely to begin their trip in Boston, the following route summaries describe how to reach each of the three itineraries. As your state loop will always start and end at the same point, simply reverse the routes to return to Boston.

To Maine

Exit airport and follow SR 1A north three miles to SR 60 (Squire Road); two miles to US 1. North on US 1 for nine miles to I-95. North on I-95 for approximately 48 miles to Kittery, a stop on the Maine itinerary.

To New Hampshire

While you could follow the above and join the New Hampshire route along the coast, it's quicker to use this route:

From the airport take the Sumner and Callahan Tunnels to I-93 north for 34 miles. This is the first exit in New Hampshire (SR 38). Go east one mile to SR 28 and then north a mile to Salem, a stop on the New Hampshire itinerary.

To Vermont

Take the Sumner and Callahan Tunnels to I-93 south to the Massachusetts Turnpike (I-90) westbound for 10 miles to I-95 north. Stay on I-95 for six miles to SR 2 west. Take SR 2 for 80 miles to I-91 and then travel north for 17 miles to the first exit in Vermont (Exit 1). In another mile you're in Brattleboro, a stop on the Vermont itinerary.

Addendum 2

Quick Reference Attraction Index

This is an alphabetical listing of all attractions, with the page number, hours, and fees. The hours shown are for the summer months, generally June through September. If traveling at other times of the year it is a good idea to check for closures or reduced hours. When no times are given, the attraction is open all day, at least during daylight hours. Visitor centers in national and state parks or forests are usually open from 8:00 or 9:00 a.m. until at least 5:00 p.m., although the parks themselves do not close or have much longer hours.

The cost indicated is the full adult admission price, rounded up to the next dollar, based on prices at time of publication. Thus, these figures are for reference purposes only. Discounts for children or senior citizens are usually available. National and state parks generally do not have a per person admission price, but there is a fee for each car entering. This is waived in the case of national parks for persons who present a Golden Eagle or Golden Age Passport. Areas implementing this type of fee structure are indicated by a dollar sign ($) in the listing without a specific amount. The letter "D" indicates donations in lieu of a fixed admission price.

MAINE

Attraction/Hours	Cost	Page
Acadia National Park	$	25
Acadian Village, daily 12-5	3	42
Acadian Whale Watcher, 6 departures daily	19-29	27
Acadia Zoo, daily 9:30-Dusk	5	28
Androscoggin Historical Society Museum Mon-Fri 1:30-5	D	19
Aquaboggen Water Park, daily 10-6	22	14
Atlantic Seal Cruises, daily at 9:30, 1:30 & 6	20	35
Augusta State Park	Free	20
Bald Head Cliff	Free	17
Bangor Historical Society Museum, Mon-Fri 12-4	2	28

Attraction/Hours	Cost	Page
Bates College	Free	20
Baxter State Park	$	40
Bay View Cruises, daily 10:30-6:30	8	11
Black House, Mon-Sat 10-4	5	28
Blaine House, Mon-Fri 2-4	D	20
Boothbay Railway Village, daily 9:30-5	5	28
Bowdoin College, museum hours vary	D (mus.)	34
Brick Store Museum, Tue-Sat 10-4:30	4	15
Burnham Tavern Museum, Mon-Fri 10-5	2	24
Camden Hills State Park	Free	30
Cape Neddick Lighthouse	Free	17
Caribou Historical Museum, Tue-Sat	D	42
Cascade Water and Amusement Park		
daily 10-10	15	14
Casco Bay Lines, daily 10-3	10	11
Castle Tucker Historic Museum,		
Tue-Sat 11-4	3	33
Children's Museum of Maine		
Tue-Sat 10-5;		
Sun-Mon 12-5	4	10
Colby College, museum hours vary	Free	20
Cole Land Transportation Museum,		
daily 9-5	2	29
Colonial Pemaquid State Historic Site,		
Mon-Sat 10-5; Sun 11-5	D	43
Desert of Maine, daily 9-dusk	5	35
Dock Square	Free	15
Dr. Moses Mason House, Mon-Fri 10-4	2	38
Dyer Library and York Institute Museum		
Tue-Fri 10-5; Sat 9-noon	2	14
East Point Sanctuary	Free	14
Farnsworth Art Museum,		
Mon-Sat 10-5; Sun 1-5	5	31
Finestkind Scenic Cruises, daily;		
inquire for schedule	7-11	16
Fish and Wildlife Visitor Center, daily 10-4	3	18
Fort Edgecomb State Historic Site, daily 9-5	1	33
Fort Foster, daily 9-5	2	17
Fort Kent State Historic Site	D	42
Fort Knox State Historic Site, daily 9-dusk	2	29
Fort McClary State Historic Site, daily 9-dusk	1	17
Fort Popham State Historic Site, daily 9-dusk	Free	43
Fort Western Museum on the Kennebec		
Mon-Fri 10-5; Sat-Sun 1-5	4	20
Fort William Henry State Historic Site		
daily 9-dusk	1	43
Fraser Paper Ltd., Mon-Fri 9, 10,		
11, 1, 2 & 3	Free	42
Gardens of Vesper Hill Children's Chapel		
daily 10-4	D	31
Georges River Canal System	Free	31
Gilley Museum, Tue-Sun 10-5	3	27
Gilsland Farm, Mon-Sat 9-5;		
Sun 12-5	Free	36

Attraction/Hours	Cost	Page
Grafton Notch State Park	Free	38
Hamilton House, Tue, Thu, Sat-Sun 12-4	4	17
Hamlin Memorial Library and Gallery, Mon-Fri 10-5	D	38
Hardy III Boat Tour, daily at 9, 4:30, 6 & 8:30	7-26	43
Harvey Butler Rhododendron Sanctuary	Free	18
Houston Brook Falls	Free	21
Hunter Cove Sanctuary	Free	39
Jones Museum of Glass and Ceramics Mon-Sat 10-5; Sun 1-5	4	37
Josephine Newman Sanctuary	Free	43
Katahdin/Moosehead Marine Museum Tue-Sun 11-2; Museum daily 9-5	D (Mus.)	22
Kennebunkport Maritime Museum and Gallery, Mon-Sat 10-5; Sun 11-4	2	16
Kittery Historical and Naval Museum Mon-Fri 10-4	3	17
Lighthouse Park	Free	43
Lumberman's Museum, Tue-Sat 10-4; Sun 12-4	3	42
Maine Coast Artists Gallery, daily 10-5	D	30
Maine Coast Navigation and Railroad Train: 11. 1 & 3; Boat: 11:30, 1:30 & 3:30	8 each	33
Maine Maritime Museum, daily 9:30-5	6	34
Maine State Building and All Souls Chapel daily 9-1	1	18
Maine State Museum, Mon-Fri 9-5; Sat 10-5; Sun 1-4	2	20
Maine Yankee Energy Information Center Mon-Sat 10-5; Sun 12-4	Free	33
Margaret Chase Smith Library, Mon-Fri 10-4	D	21
Marrett House, Tue, Thu, Sat-Sun 12-4	4	36
Merryspring, daily 9-6	Free	30
Monmouth Museum, Tue-Sun 1-4	3	19
Montpelier, Wed-Sun 9-5:30	3	31
Moosehorn National Wildlife Refuge	Free	23
Mount Desert Oceanarium, Mon-Sat 9-5	5	27
Moxie Falls	Free	22
Musical Wonder House, daily 10-5	10	33
Neal Dow Memorial, Mon-Fri 11-4	D	11
Nickels-Sortwell House, Wed-Sun 12-4	4	33
Nordica Homestead Museum, Tue-Sat 10-5; Sun 1-5	2	39
Norlands Living History Center, daily 10-4	5	38
North American Wildlife Expo, daily 9-9	4	35
Nylander Museum, Wed-Sun 1-5	D	41
Ogunquit Museum of American Art Mon-Fri 10:30-5	D	16
Old Conway House and Museum, Tue-Fri 10-4	2	30
Old Lincoln County Jail and Museum, Tue-Sun 11-4:30	2	33

Attraction/Hours	Cost	Page
Old Post Exchange	Free	10
Old Town Museum, Wed-Sun 1-5	D	29
Old York, Tue-Sat 10-5	6	16
Owls Head Transportation Museum, daily 10-5	4	31
Pejepscot Museum and Skolfield-Whittier House		
Mon-Fri 10-3; Sat 1-4	D	34
Penobscot Marine Museum, Mon-Sat 9:30-5;		
Sun 1-5	5	29
Perham's of West Paris, daily 9-5	Free	38
Perkins Arboretum and Bird Sanctuary	Free	21
Pierce Park	Free	41
Portland Head Light, daily 10-4	2	13
Portland Museum of Art, Tue-Sat 10-5;		
Sun 12-5	4	10
Portland Observatory, Wed, Thu, Sun 1-5;		
Fri-Sat 10-5	2	11
Pownalborough Courthouse, Wed-Sat 10-4;		
Sun 12-4	3	33
Presque Isle State Park	$	41
Quoddy Head State Park, daily 9-dusk	2	24
Rachel Carson National Wildlife Refuge	D	15
Rangely Lakes State Park	$	39
Redington Museum, Tue-Sat 10-2	3	21
Rockport Marine Park	Free	30
Roosevelt Campobello International Park		
daily 9-5	Free	24
Round Top Center for the Arts, daily 10-4	D	31
Ruggles House, Mon-Sat 9:30-4:30; Sun 11-4:30	2	25
St. Andrew's	Free	32
St. Patrick's Church, daily 9-dusk	D	32
Sarah Orne Jewett House, Tue, Thu,		
Sat-Sun 12-4	4	17
Scarborough Marsh Nature Center		
daily 9:30-5:30	Free	13
	Tours 6	
Schoodic Point (Acadia National Park)	Free	25
Seashore Trolley Museum, daily 10-5:30	6	15
Seal Cove Auto Museum, daily 10-5	5	28
Shaker Museum, Mon-Sat 10-4:30	4-6	18
Shore Village Museum, daily 10-4	D	31
Silverlining, daily 10, 12:30, 3 & 5:30	25	16
Songo River Queen II		
Long: daily 9:45 & 3:45	9	37
Short: daily 1, 2:30 & 7	6	
Southworth Planetarium, Mon-Fri 9-5	4	11
Spring Point Museum, Wed-Sun 1-4	2	13
Stanley Museum, Tue-Sun 1-4	2	40
Stanwood Homestead Museum &		
Bird Sanctuary; Museum daily 10-4	3	28
Statehouse, Mon-Fri 8-5	Free	20
Tate House, Tue, Sat 10-4; Sun 1-4	3	11
Thomas Heritage House, by appt.	2	42
Thorncrag Bird Sanctuary	Free	19

Attraction/Hours	*Cost*	*Page*
Two Lights State Park	Free	13
University of Maine	Free	29
Vaughan Woods, daily 9am-8pm	1	17
Victoria Mansion, Tue-Sat 11-4; Sun 1-5	4	12
Wadsworth-Longfellow House, Tue-Sat 10-4	4	10
Waldoboro Museum, daily 1-4:30	D	31
Waponahki Museum, Mon-Fri 8:30-11		
& 12:30-3:30	D	23
Waterfront Heritage Park	Free	30
Wells Auto Museum, daily 10-4	4	15
Wells National Estuarine Research Reserve		
daily 8-5	3	15
Wilhelm Reich Museum, Tue-Sun 1-5	3	39
Yarmouth Historical Society		
Museum of History, Tue-Sat 10-5	D	35

NEW HAMPSHIRE

Abbot-Spalding House Museum		
Sat 1-4 & by appointment	Free	53
American Independence Museum		
Tue-Sat 10-4; Sun 12-4	4	46
America's Stonehenge, daily 9-5	7	42
Anheuser-Busch, daily 9:30-5	Free	53
Attitash Alpine Slide, daily 10-6	6-15	60
Audubon-Paradise Point Nature Center		
daily 10-5	D	71
Barrett House, Thu-Sun 12-4	4	70
Basin, The	Free	65
Cannon Mountain Aerial Tramway II		
daily 9-7 (4:30 until July 4 &		
after Labor Day)	9	64
Canobie Lake Park, daily noon-10	14	52
Canterbury Shaker Village, Mon-Sat 10-5;		
Sun 12-5	8	67
Castle in the Clouds, daily 10-5	4-10	71
Cathedral of the Pines, daily 9-5	D	70
Centre Franco-Americain, Mon-Fri 8-4;		
Sat 9:30-1	D	46
Charlestown Historic District	Free	55
Children's Museum of Portsmouth		
Mon-Sat 10-5; Sun 1-5	4	50
Christa McAuliffe Planetarium		
Tue-Fri 2 & 3:30; Sat-Sun12:30, 2 & 3:30	5	67
Claremont Society Museum, Sun-Fri 2-5	Free	55
Clark's Trading Post, daily 9-5:45	7	58
Coach and Eagle Trail	Free	68
Conservation Center	Free	67
Conway Scenic Railroad, daily 10, 12, 2 & 4	8	59
Crawford Notch State Park	Free	60
Currier Gallery of Art, Tue-Sat 10-4; Sun 1-5	Free	46
Daniel Webster Birthplace, daily 10-6	3	66
Dartmouth College, museum hours vary	Free	56

Attraction/Hours	Cost	Page
Dixville Notch	Free	63
Echo Lake (Franconia Notch)	Free	64
Echo Lake State Park, daily 9-8	3	59
Florence Hyde Speare Memorial Building		
Tue, Thu 10-4; Wed 10-3; Sat 1-4	2	53
Flume, The, daily 9-4:30	6	65
Fort at Number Four Living History Museum		
Wed-Mon 10-4	6	55
Fort Constitution Historic Site, daily 9-4	2	51
Fort Stark Historic Site, daily 9-4	2	51
Foundation for Biblical Research,		
Tue-Sat 10-4	D	55
Franconia Notch/Franconia Notch State Park	Free	64
Frost Place, Wed-Mon 1-5	3	64
Frye's Measure Mill, Tue-Sat 10-5; Sun noon-5	3	53
Fuller Gardens, daily 10-6	4	52
Gilman Garrison House, Tue, Thu, Sat-Sun 12-5	4	46
Governor John Wentworth Historic Site, daily 9-4	2	72
Grand Manor Car Museum, daily 9:30-5	5	59
Great Bay National Estuarine		
Research Reserve	Free	69
Hampshire Pewter Company, Mon-Fri		
hourly 9-3	Free	72
Heritage-New Hampshire, daily 9-6	8	60
Hobo Railroad, daily 11, 1, 3, 5 & 7		
(Only 11 & 1 in June)	7	58
Horatio Colony Museum, Tue-Sat 11-4	Free	54
Isle of Shoals Steamship Company,		
daily 11 & 2	35	51
Jackson House, Sat 1-4	4	50
Jaffrey Historic District,		
Melville Academy Museum, Sat-Sun 2-4	D	69
John Paul Jones House, Mon-Sat 10-4; Sun 12-4	4	49
Kancamagus Highway	Free	58
Kimbal Jenkins Estate, Tue-Sat 10-4	5	68
Langdon House, Wed-Sun 12-5	4	49
LaSalette Shrine	Free	56
Lawrence Lee Scouting Museum, daily 10-4	Free	46
Libby Museum, Tue-Sun 10-4	1	72
Library Arts Center, Sat-Sun 10-5	Free	70
Loon Montain Park, daily 9-5	8	58
Lost River, daily 9-6	7	57
Manchester Historic Association		
Tue-Fri 9-4; Sat 10-4	Free	46
Manchester Institute of Arts and Sciences		
Mon-Sat 9-5	Free	46
Mary Baker Eddy Historic House		
Tue-Sat 10-5; Sun 2-5	2	71
Miller State Park, daily 10-6	3	54
Monadnock State Park	3	69
Moore Station and Dam, daily 9-5	Free	63
Mt. Kearsage Indian Museum,		
Mon-Sat 10-5: Sun 1-5	5	70
Mt. Sunapee State Park	3	70

Attraction/Hours	Cost	Page
Mount Washington Auto Road, daily 7:30-6	5-18	62
Mount Washington Cog Railway,		
daily 9-4 (on the hour)	35	61
MS Mount Washington, daily 9, 12 & 3:30	11-13	66
Museum at Lower Shaker Village		
Mon-Sat 10-5; Sun 12-5	4	56
Museum of Childhood at Wakefield		
Mon, Wed-Sat 11-4; Sun 1-4	3	72
Museum of New Hampshire History		
Mon-Fri 9-4:30; Sat-Sun 12-4:30	D	68
MV Judge Sewall, Mon-Fri 11:30,		
1:30 & 3:30; Sat-Sun 10 & 12	6	72
MV Mount Sunapee, daily 10 & 2:30	9	70
Nansen Wayside Park	Free	62
Nestlenook Farm, daily 9-5	Free	60
	(ride fees)	
New England Ski Museum, Thu-Tue 12-5	Free	65
New Hampshire Seacoast Cruises		
Whale Watch: daily 8am		
Islands: daily 2:30	9-22	51
Odiorne Point State Park	3	51
Old Man of the Mountain	Free	65
Opera House (Claremont),		
inquire for schedule at box office	Vary	55
Original Golden Pond Tours		
daily 10:30, 1:30 & 3:30	8	66
Peterborough Historical Society and Museum		
Mon-Sat 10-4	1	54
Pierce Manse, Mon-Fri 11-3	2	68
Pinkham Notch,	Free	62
Polar Ice Caves, daily 9-5	9	65
Port of Portsmouth Maritime Msm./		
Alvacore Park, daily 9:30-5	4	50
Portsmouth Harbor Cruises		
Mon-Fri 12 & 2; Sat-Sun 10, 12 & 3	7-12	51
Prescott Park	Free	49
Rhododendron State Park	3	69
Rollins State Park, daily 9am-8pm	3	71
Ruggles Mine, daily 9-5	10	57
Rundlet-May House, Wed-Sun 12-5	4	49
Saint-Gaudens National Historic Site		
daily 8:30-4:30	2	55
Sandwich Hist. Society and		
Elisha Marston House, Tue-Sat 11-5	D	71
Santa's Village, daily 9:30-6:30	12	62
Science Center of New Hampshire		
daily 9:30-4:30	6	66
Seabrook Station Science and Nature Center		
Mon-Sat 10-4	Free	52
Seacoast Science Center,		
Tue-Sun 10-5; Mon 12-5	3	51
Shieling State Forest	Free	54
Shrine of Our Lady of Grace, daily	Free	63
Silver Ranch Airpark, daily 9-5	8-40	70

Attraction/Hours	Cost	Page
Six Gun City, daily 9-6	10	61
Squam Lake Tours, daily 10, 2 & 4	10	66
State House, Mon-Fri 8-4:30	Free	67
Storyland, daily 9-6	14	59
Strawberry Banke Museum, daily 10-5	8	49
Sugar Hill Historical Museum,		
Thu, Sat-Sun 1-4 & by appt.	2	71
Urban Forestry Center	Free	50
Warner House, Tue-Sat 10-4; Sun 1-4	4	49
Water Country, daily 9:30-7:30	18	50
Weeks State Park, Wed-Sun 10-6	3	63
Wentworth-Coolidge Mansion, daily 10-5	3	50
Wentworth-Gardner House, Tue-Sun 1-4	4	50
Whale's Tale Water Park, daily 10-6	14	58
Wildcat Mountain Gondola Tramway		
daily 10-4:15	8	62
Wolfboro Historical Society Museum		
Mon-Sat 10-4	D	72
Woodman Institute, Tue-Sat 2-5	D	69
Wright Museum-A Museum of		
American Enterprise,		
Mon-Sat 10-5; Sun 12-5	5	72
Wyman Tavern Museum, Thu-Sat 11-4	2	54
Zimmeman House, by reservation	6	46

VERMONT

American Maple Products Company		
Mon-Fri 8-4	Free	79
American Museum of Fly Fishing, daily 10-4	2	88
Basketville, daily 9-5	Free	86
Battery Park	Free	74
Ben and Jerry's Ice Cream Factory,		
tours daily 9am-8pm	1	81
Bennington Battle Monument, daily 9-5	1	87
Bennington Museum, daily 9-5	5	87
Billings Farm and Museum, daily 10-5	6	83
Birds of Vermont Museum, Wed-Mon 10-4	4	92
Black River Academy Museum,		
Wed-Sun 12-4	D	85
Brattleboro Museum and Arts Center		
Tue-Sun 12-6	2	86
Bread and Puppet Museum, daily 10-6	D	80
Cabot Creamery, Mon-Sat 9-5; Sun 11-4	1	80
Catamount Brewing Company		
Mon-Sat 11, 1 & 3; Sun 1 & 3	Free	84
Church Street Marketplace	Free	74
Cold Hollow Cider Mill, daily 8-7	Free	81
Dakin Farm, daily 9-5	Free	91
Dana House, Mon-Sat 10-5; Sun 2-5	4	83
Danforth's Sugarhouse, daily 9-4:30	Free	81
Ethan Allen Homestead,		
Mon-Sat 10-5; Sun 1-5	4	74

Attraction/Hours	Cost	Page
Ethan Allen Park, Tower Wed-Sun 12-8	Free	74
Factory Marketplace at Kennedy Brothers		
daily 9-6	Free	90
Fairbanks Museum and Planetarium		
Mon-Sat 10-6; Sun 1-5	4-6	80
Granville Gulf State Park	Free	82
Green Mountain Flyer, daily 11 & 2	10	85
Green Mountain National Forest:	All free	82
(Falls of Lana, Mt. Horrid Observation Site,		
Robert Frost Trail, Robert Frost Wayside,		
Texas Falls Recreation Area, White Rocks)		
Guild of Old Time Crafts and Industries		
Wed-Sun 10-5	Free	85
Haskell Free Library and Opera House,		
Tue-Wed 10-5;	Free	79
Thu-Sat 1-5	(Opera fee)	
Hildene, daily 9:30-4	6	88
Hubbardton Battlefield and Museum		
Wed-Sun 9:30-5:30	Free	93
Hyde Log Cabin, Wed-Sun 11-5	1	75
Jay Peak Resort, daily 10-5	6	92
Joseph Cerniglia Winery, daily 10-5	Free	84
Joseph Smith Birthplace Memorial, daily 9-7	Free	93
Justin Smith Morrill Homestead,		
Wed-Sun 9:30-5:30	Free	93
Killington Ski and Summer Resort, daily 10-4	4	83
Lake Champlain Maritime Museum		
daily 10-5	3	90
LaMoille Valley Railroad		
1-hr. trip: daily 12:15 & 3:30;		
2-hr. trip: daily 10 & 1:30	10-15	78
Mary Bryan Art Gallery, daily 11-5	Free	77
Missiquoi National Wildlife Refuge	Free	77
Montshire Museum of Science, daily 10-5	5	93
Morrisville Noyes House Historical Museum		
Wed-Sat 12-5	Free	78
Morse Farm and Sugarhouse, daily 8-6	Free	81
Mount Equinox, daily 8am-10pm	$	88
Mount Independence, daily 9:30-5:30	Free	94
Mount Mansfield State Park	Free	77
Mount Snow Ski Area, Sat-Sun 9-3	7	86
New England Maple Museum, daily 8:30-5:30	2	89
Norman Rockwell Exhibit, daily 9-5	1	87
Norman Rockwell Museum of Vermont		
daily 9-6	3	89
Norwich University Museum, Mon-Fri 9-5	Free	93
Old Constitution House, Wed-Sun 10-4	1	84
Old First Church, Mon-Sat 10-4; Sun 1-4	D	87
Old Rockingham Meeting House, daily 10-4	1	85
Old Round Church, daily 10-4	D	92
Old Stone House Museum, daily 11-5	3	79
Original Maple Grove Museum and Factory		
Mon-Fri 8-4:30	1	80
Park McCullough House, daily 10-4	4	87

Attraction/Hours	Cost	Page
Pico Alpine Slide, daily 10-6	4	83
Plymouth Notch Historic District/		
Birthplace of Calvin Coolidge		
daily 9:30-5:30	4	83
Quechee Gorge	Free	84
Robert H. Fleming Museum		
Tue-Fri 9-4; Sat-Sun 1-5	D	74
Rock of Ages, daily 8:30-5	Free	81
Rokeby Museum,		
Wed-Sun at 11, 12:30 & 2	4	90
Royal Lipizzan Stallions of Austria		
Call for schedule & prices		75
St. Albans Historical Museum, Tue-Sat 1-4	2	77
St. Anne's Shrine	Free	75
St. Johnsbury Athenaeum Art Gallery		
Mon-Fri 10-5:30; Sat 9:30-4	D	80
Santa's Land, daily 9:30-4:30	8	86
Shelburne Farms,		
daily 9:30, 11, 12:30, 2 & 3:30	7	91
Shelburne Museum, daily 10-5	15	91
Sheldon Museum, Mon-Fri 10-5; Sat 10-4	4	90
Simon Pearce Glass Works, daily 9-5	Free	84
Smugglers Notch State Park	Free	77
Southern Vermont Art Center		
Tue-Sat 10-5; Sun 12-5	3	88
Spirit of Ethan Allen, daily 10, 12, 2 & 4	8	74
State Capitol, Mon-Fri 8-4; Sat 11-2:30	Free	81
Stellefane Society Museum		
daily 6pm & by reservation	Free	85
Stowe Alpine Slide, daily 10-5	6	78
Stowe Auto Road, daily 10-5	$	78
Stowe Gondola, daily 10-5	9	78
Stowe Recreation Path	Free	78
Stratton Arts Festival		
daily (during season) 10-5	6	94
Sugarbush Farms		
Mon-Fri 7:30-4; Sat-Sun 9:30-4	Free	83
Sugarmill Farm and Museum		
daily 8am-8pm	5	79
Timber Village, daily	Free	
	(ride fees)	84
UVM Morgan Horse Farm, daily 9-4	4	90
Vermont Country Store		
Mon-Sat 9-5; Sun 10-5	Free	85
Vermont Historical Society		
Tue-Fri 9-4:30; Sat 9-4; Sun12-4	3	81
Vermont Marble Exhibit, daily 9-5:30	4	89
Vermont Raptor Center, daily 10-4	5	83
Vermont Teddy Bear Company		
Mon-Sat 10-4; Sun 11-4	Free	91
Vermont Wildflower Farm, daily 10-5	3	91
Westminster MG Car Museum, Sat-Sun 10-5	4	94
Wilson Castle, daily 9-6	6	89

Addendum 3

General State Information

MAINE

Maine Publicity Bureau
P.O. Box 2300
Hallowell, ME 04347-2300
(800) 323-6330
(207) 623-0363

NEW HAMPSHIRE

Office of Travel and Tourism
172 Pembroke Road
Concord, NH 03302
(800) 386-4664
(603) 271-2666
Fall Foliage Reports (Sept-Oct): (800) 258-3608

VERMONT

Vermont Travel Division
Agency of Development and Community Affairs
134 State Street
Montpelier, VT 05602
(802) 828-2648

National Park/Forest Service Facilities

Address all written inquires to the Superintendent (Parks) or Forest Supervisor of the particular facility at the address given.

MAINE

Acadia National Park
Bar Harbor, ME 04609
(207) 288-3338

NEW HAMPSHIRE

White Mountain National Forest
P.O. Box 638
Laconia, NH 03247
(603) 528-8721

VERMONT

Green Mountain National Forest
P.O. Box 519
Rutland, VT 05702
(802) 773-0300

Lodging

MAJOR HOTEL CHAINS
Toll Free Reservation and Information Numbers:

Best Western International	(800) 528-1234
Choice Hotels:	
Clarion Hotels, Comfort Inn,	
Quality Inn, Rodeway Inn	(800) 221-2222
EconoLodge, Friendship Inns	(800) 424-4777
Days Inns	(800) 325-2525
Hilton Hotels	(800) 445-8667
Holiday Inns	(800) 465-4329
Howard Johnson Motor Lodges	(800) 446-4656
Marriott Hotels:	
Courtyards By Marriott	(800) 321-2211
Fairfield Inns	(800) 228-2800
Marriott Hotels & Resorts	(800) 228-9290

Residence Inns By Marriott	(800) 331-3131
Ramada Inns	(800) 228-2828
Sheraton Hotels	(800) 325-3535
Super 8	(800) 843-1991
Suisse Chalet	(800) 258-1980
Travelodge	(800) 255-3050

The following list shows the locations of chains with a significant presence in Maine, New Hampshire and Vermont. If there is more than one property at a location this is indicated by an asterisk (*). Only chains with six or more locations are shown.

BEST WESTERN

Maine
Augusta, Bangor, Bar Harbor, Bucksport, Millinocket, Orono, Portland

New Hampshire
Exeter, Glen, Keene, North Conway

Vermont
Bennington, Ludlow, Mt. Snow, Rutland

CHOICE
Comfort Inns/Quality Inns/Clarion Hotels

Maine
Auburn, Augusta, Bangor, Bar Harbor, Brunswick, Ellsworth, Kennebunkport, Kingfield, Portland

New Hampshire
Ashland, Concord, Nashua*, Portsmouth

Vermont
Burlington*, Killington, Montpelier, Quechee, Rutland, White River Junction

Econolodge/Friendship Inns

Maine
Bangor*, Brewer, Brunswick, Kennebunk, Millinocket, Portland, Presque Isle, Waterville

New Hampshire
Concord, Dover, Manchester, Rochester

Vermont
Burlington*, Montpelier, Quechee, Mendon, St. Albans, Shelburne

DAYS INN

Maine
Augusta, Bangor, Bar Harbor, Caribou, Kittery, Portland, Trenton

New Hampshire
Concord, Dover, Keene, Lebanon, Manchester, North Conway, Nashua, Plymouth

Vermont
Barre, Brattleboro, Colchester (Burlington area), Lyndonville, Rutland, Shelburne

HOLIDAY INNS

Maine
Augusta, Bangor*, Bar Harbor, Bath, Ellsworth, Portland*, Waterville

New Hampshire
Concord, Manchester, Nashua, Portsmouth

Vermont
Burlington, Rutland, Waterbury, White River Junction

HOWARD JOHNSON

Maine
Bangor, Portland*, Waterville

New Hampshire
Manchester, Nashua, Portsmouth

Vermont
Barre, Burlington*, Rutland, Springfield, White River Junction

MARRIOTT
Fairfield Inns

Maine
Bangor, Bar Harbor, Scarborough

New Hampshire
Merrimack

Vermont
Colchester (Burlington area)

Marriott Hotels and Resorts

Maine
Bangor, Portland

New Hampshire
Nashua

Residence Inns

New Hampshire
Nashua

Vermont
Burlington

RAMADA INNS

Maine
Bangor, Lewiston, Portland

New Hampshire
Merrimack

Vermont
Bennington, Burlington

SUPER 8

Maine
Augusta, Bangor, Brunswick, Freeport, Lewiston, Sanford, Westbrook

New Hampshire
Keene, Manchester, Tilton (Laconia)

Vermont
Brattleboro, Newport, White River Junction

SUISSE CHALET

Maine
Augusta, Portland*

New Hampshire
Manchester, Plymouth, Portsmouth, Salem

Vermont
Williston

National Car Rental Companies

Alamo	(800) 327-9633
Avis	(800) 321-1212
Budget	(800) 527-0700
Dollar	(800) 421-6868
Enterprise	(800) 325-8007
Hertz	(800) 654-3131
National	(800) 227-7368
Thrifty	(800) 367-2277

Other Information

While all three northern New England states provide excellent opportunities for whitewater rafting and all except Vermont are popular places for whale watching (and for seeing the colorful Atlantic puffins), the best places for both are in Maine. The lists below are not all-inclusive, but represent a sampling of operators.

WHALE AND PUFFIN WATCHING CRUISES

Only those operators who share proceeds with the National Audubon Society are listed.

Atlantic Expeditions
St. George, ME 04857
(207) 372-8621

Cap'n Fish Boat Cruises
Boothbay Harbor, ME 04538
(207) 633-3244

Hardy Boat Cruises
New Harbor, ME 04554
(207) 677-2026

Northeast Cruises
Seal Harbor, ME 04675
(207) 276-5803

WHITEWATER RAFTING

The best rafting is in the Forks, where these operators are located.

Access to Adventure
PO Box T
Brunswick, ME 04011
(800) 864-2676

Adventure River Expeditions
PO Box 101, Route 201
The Forks, ME 04985
(800) 765-7238

Crab Apple Whitewater, Inc.
HC 63, Box 25, Route 201
The Forks, ME 04985
(800) 553-7238

Downeast Whitewater Rafting Inc.
Box 119, Route 302
Center Conway, NH 03813
(800) 677-RAFT

Magic Falls Rafting Company
PO Box 9
W. Forks, ME 04985
(800) 207-RAFT

Moxie Outdoor Adventures
Lake Moxie Camps
The Forks, ME 04985
(800) 866-6943

North American Whitewater Expeditions
PO Box 64
West Forks, ME 04925
(800) 727-4379

Northern Outdoors Inc.
PO Box 100, Route 201
The Forks, ME 04985
(800) 765-RAFT

Professional River Runners of Maine, Inc.
PO Box 92, Route 201
West Forks, ME 04985
(800) 325-3911

Operating season varies by company, but generally runs from April through October. Different trips are available, most on a daily basis, varying from half- and full-day excursions to multi-day adventures. The above operators are licensed and provide all necessary protective equipment to keep you dry (relatively speaking) and safe. Unless you have special protective gear for your camera, it's urged that you don't bring one with you.

MISCELLANEOUS

For information on wilderness adventures in Baxter State Park, including camping reservations, write:

Baxter State Park
64 Balsam Drive
Millinocket, ME 04462